THE BORK HEARINGS

The Bork Hearings

Highlights from the Most Controversial Judicial Confirmation Battle in U.S. History

Edited by
Ralph E. Shaffer

 Markus Wiener Publishers
Princeton

Second printing, 2021

For information write to:
Markus Wiener Publishers
231 Nassau Street, Princeton, NJ 08542
www.markuswiener.com

Library of Congress Cataloging-in-Publication Data

The Bork hearings : highlights from the most controversial judicial
confirmation battle in U.S. history / edited by Ralph E. Shaffer
p. cm.
Includes bibliographical references.
ISBN 978-1-55876-374-6 (hardcover : alk. paper)
ISBN 978-1-55876-375-3 (pbk. : alk. paper)
1. United States. Supreme Court—Officials and employees—Selection
and appointment. 2. Judges—Selection and appointment—United States.
3. Bork, Robert H. 4. Political questions and judicial power—United States.
I. Shaffer, Ralph E.
KF8742.B67 2005
347.73'2634—dc22   2005014530

CONTENTS

PREFACE

On a Saturday afternoon in September, 1987, after four and a half days of rigorous questioning by members of the Senate Judiciary Committee, Robert H. Bork was finally asked why he wanted to serve on the United States Supreme Court. That question came from a committee member very supportive of Bork's nomination, Wyoming's Alan Simpson. With the nomination in doubt, Simpson may have wondered why anyone would want a post so dearly that the nominee would subject himself to such a severe inquisition from his critics. The answer Bork offered is one any constitutional lawyer or judge could readily agree with and would become the most memorable line served up to a nationwide television and radio audience during that week.

> Senator, I guess the answer to that is that I have spent my life in intellectual pursuits in the law, and since I have been a judge I particularly like the courtroom. I liked the courtroom as an advocate, and I like the courtroom as a judge, and I enjoy the give and take and the intellectual effort involved....
>
> [A]nd that is, of course, the court that has the most interesting cases and issues, and I think it would be an intellectual feast just to be there and to read the briefs and discuss things with counsel and discuss things with my colleagues....

To most Americans who watched the proceedings, and to Senator Simpson, the hearings themselves were an "intellectual feast." But not for Bork. In *The Tempting of America*, written after rejection of his nomination, he dismissed the popular view that the nation witnessed and heard "a weighty discussion of constitutional theory."

Readers of the pages that follow will judge for themselves the merit of the discussion. Editing has eliminated repetitive questions and their repetitive answers, and telescoped fundamentally essential but differing views of the constitution spread over most of a week and nearly 900 pages, into a serious debate on some of the great constitutional issues of 1987— issues that remain serious matters of contention for later generations.

Whenever future nominees for the highest court in the land prepare for their own hearings, this little volume will be there as a testament to the probing that may await them.

INTRODUCTION

The retirement of Associate Justice Lewis Powell at the end of the Supreme Court's 1986–87 term sparked the most stimulating public debate about the meaning of the Constitution in recent memory. Appropriately, it occurred as the nation celebrated the two hundredth anniversary of that document. While the attention of most Americans focused on the bicentennial hoopla and pageantry in Philadelphia and New York, they were at the same time riveted to a drama unfolding in Washington. There, under the probing eye of network television, the nation was treated to a penetrating, in-depth argument about the interpretation and functioning of the national charter. Not since the tumultuous states' rights controversy before the Civil War had so many prominent politicians and legal scholars been embroiled in a discussion of this nature.

The vehicle for the debate was the testimony presented to the Senate Judiciary Committee in the last two weeks of September, 1987, as the committee prepared a recommendation to the full Senate on President Ronald Reagan's nomination to fill the Powell vacancy. Even before the hearings had ended, it was apparent to those following the live telecasts that they had witnessed a unique event in the nation's history.

This view was shared by conservatives and liberals alike. Republican Senator Orrin Hatch, one of the leading participants in the hearings held to confirm Powell's replacement, told the nominee, who was on the witness stand on Constitution Day, that his analysis of how the

Constitution works was unequaled by any commentator or television program.

To fellow Republican Alan Simpson the four and a half days that the committee grilled the nominee were like a return to law school, with the sharpest kid in class debating the sharpest law professor in the country. Democrat Patrick Leahy saw the hearing as a graduate seminar in constitutional law.

When the nominee finished his testimony, former Attorney General William Rogers called the proceedings an adult education class of the highest order, "one that ought to be made required reading for law students."

The importance of Powell's seat on the Court justified such a high-level debate. On an evenly divided court, Powell often held a swing vote and was referred to by one commentator as the most important man in America. His successor would inherit that position.

From a court that had been decisively liberal at the start of the Nixon years, a changing membership had moved the justices closer to a conservative majority. By 1987 Reagan had made three appointments — two new justices and the elevation of an Associate Justice to Chief Justice. The new appointees, Antonin Scalia and Sandra Day O'Connor, were conservatives who joined with Justice Byron White and Chief Justice William Rehnquist for an almost immovable block of four. Opposed to them were three aging liberals — William Brennan, Thurgood Marshall, and Harry Blackmun — who could often summon support from a fourth justice, John Paul Stevens. The Powell seat thus held the balance of power.

On July 1, 1987, Reagan announced the nomination of Robert Bork to fill the Powell vacancy. Passed over the previous year when Scalia had been nominated to replace Warren Burger, Bork was not an unexpected nominee. He had served on the Federal Court of Appeals for the District of Columbia Circuit since 1982, and his writings as a law professor and his opinions on the court endeared him to conservatives.

Had he been nominated the previous year, when liberals concentrated their attack on the elevation of Rehnquist to Chief Justice, he might have been confirmed without a struggle. At that time the Judiciary Committee and the full senate were Republican controlled, with arch-conservative Strom Thurmond of South Carolina chair of the committee.

But by the time Bork was nominated the Democrats had taken control of the Senate. The new committee chair was Joseph Biden, who also was one of several Democrats seeking the party's 1988 presidential nomination.

While there was much speculation that his presidential ambitions would color Biden's direction of the confirmation hearings, that was not the case. Some of his party colleagues used the hearings for bitter attacks upon Bork, but Biden went out of his way to be courteous both in his questioning and in directing the proceedings. His presidential campaign unraveled in the course of the hearings, and within a week after Bork had left the witness stand Biden, caught in a variety of questionable actions, withdrew from the race.

Of the eight Democrats on the panel, Edward Kennedy was clearly the most abrasive and hostile questioner during the week that Bork was before the committee. Senate Majority Leader Robert Byrd was rarely present, and Paul Simon and Leahy did not press Bork to any significant extent. Howard Metzenbaum and Dennis DeConcini, sometimes joined by Howell Heflin, were responsible for the most penetrating Democratic examination of the nominee.

The most probing, insightful questioning came from Pennsylvania Republican Arlen Specter, who engaged Bork in lengthy debates on a wide-ranging field of subjects. Specter held the key vote. Uncommitted at the beginning, his questions indicated a man seeking a way to vote for confirmation without betraying the progressive social views he held.

Hatch and Thurmond offered acerbic comments from the right that tended to balance out Kennedy's caustic remarks. They formulated questions that allowed Bork to place his previous writings, which were under attack by liberals, in a more positive light, or they structured remarks so that Bork could present a modified, less troublesome position on subjects, such as minority and women's rights, that had been particularly galling to his critics. Gordon Humphrey and Charles Grassley left the direction of the Bork defense to Hatch and Thurmond, while Simpson devoted his question time to lengthy home-spun monologues that, while entertaining, contributed little to the law school atmosphere he said he so much enjoyed.

Bork went before the committee on Tuesday, September 17. The opening session that morning was devoted to "presenters," former President Gerald Ford among them, who made opening statements on behalf of the nominee. Beginning with the afternoon session that day, Bork would spend 33 hours in front of the committee before he was dismissed Saturday evening. No Supreme Court nominee had ever been examined so extensively.

The hearings continued until September 30. Dozens of witnesses appeared, individually or in panels so that the committee could hear them all. Those testifying for or against Bork included some of the most prominent legal minds in the country, including law professors Lawrence Tribe of Harvard and Edward Levi of Chicago; numerous former attorneys general, among them Griffin Bell, Nicholas Katzenbach, William French Smith, Levi, and Rogers; from the Ford administration, cabinet members William T. Coleman (Transportation) and Carla Hills (HUD); and former Chief Justice Warren Burger, whose own appointment years before had begun the process of moving the court to the right.

Although the Constitution requires confirmation of judicial appointments with the "advice and consent of the Senate," the first nominee to appear before the Judiciary Committee was Harlan F. Stone, in 1925. That practice became customary with the nomination of Felix Frankfurter in 1939. But nominees routinely refused to answer questions about judicial philosophy or the nature of the Constitution. The stock answer was that it would be improper to state views on an issue that might come before a sitting justice.

The Bork hearings departed from that routine. For the first time in the judicial confirmation process a nominee engaged in a genuine discussion of the meaning of the Constitution, the nature of the Court and its powers, and the process by which justices should interpret the law.

Simpson, near the end of Bork's fifth day before the committee, noted the difference between Bork's willingness to debate the Constitution and the attitude of other Reagan appointees. Simpson quoted Justice O'Connor: "I do not believe as a nominee I can ... criticize specific Supreme Court decisions which may well come before the Court again," and Scalia: "I do not think I should respond to the question because that may well be an issue argued before the Court and I do not want to be in the position of having ... given an indication of how I would come out on it," and Rehnquist: "I was reluctantly willing to answer your questions about the First Amendment. In effect, I must say I am very much inclined to think that I best ought not...."

Despite this closed-mouth tradition on matters of substance, Bork rarely invoked his right to remain silent on grounds that a particular issue might come before the Court. In part, that was because the committee carefully avoided questions about cases that might compromise the nominee. But when an interrogator did venture into a questionable area, Bork seemingly relished the opportunity to pursue the issue. The result was that both Bork and the committee engaged in an unprecedented discussion of constitutional theory and of Bork's previous legal opinions and academic writings.

Halfway through Bork's testimony Grassley remarked that "I do not think in the history of the Senate has a nominee been subject to this kind of questioning; and never has a judicial nominee been so forthcoming in his views." Thurmond, thinking back over his 33 years in the Senate, could not recall a nominee for any judicial position who had undergone such an intense, probing examination.

But as the hearings wound down and it became apparent to conservatives that Bork's forthright testimony had done more harm than good, the final word on the nature of the hearing may well have come from Simpson. "This will never happen again. Doesn't matter whether you are confirmed or rejected. Because the next time we have a Supreme Court nominee he or she ... will respectfully decline to give an opinion on whether any of the existing law on the Supreme Court is right or wrong."

The material that follows has been selected after a careful editing of volume one of the transcript, which contains all the questioning of Bork. The week saw four rounds of questions by the fourteen members of the panel, each of whom was allowed 30 minutes in each round. Not all members participated each time, and some used less than 30 minutes. Others, however, caught up in an exciting interchange with Bork, went beyond their allotted time.

Because of this format, a specific issue such as equal protection may have been brought up on each of the five days by several different Senators. This resulted in a great deal of repetition, both in questions and answers. To make the transcript manageable — required reading, as suggested by Rogers — the official transcript has been edited so that all questions and answers dealing with a particular subject are together.

In the pages that follow, a question from day one may actually be followed by an answer from day five. Instead of a steady stream of questions from a single Senator, the edited version reads as though it were a round table discussion, with several Senators' questions interspersed with Bork's answers. Despite the great amount of editing (the Bork testimony of questions, answers and documents covers over 850 pages alone), the text printed here does not violate either the spirit or the letter of what was said by any of the participants.

Grammatical editing has also taken place. A literal reading of the transcript reveals a great deal of broken syntax, incomplete sentences, thoughts lost in the midst of overly complicated clauses, and other problems that result when the spoken, extemporaneous word is written down verbatim. In fairness to all participants, where those problems were so noticeable as to make a reading of the manuscript difficult the editor has silently corrected the problem. Where the broken grammar was not distracting enough to cause difficulty with the reading, it has been left unchanged.

On only a few occasions has it been necessary to insert a word in order to make a complete sentence or thought. That has been done without the use of brackets or other identifying marks. Nor, when words were omitted, has the ellipsis been used, for that was done so frequently that it would be a major distraction. Since the ideas presented are what counts, anything that would impair the reader's efforts to comprehend them has been avoided. For those who wish to wade through the unedited version of the hearings, refer to part one of the official publication.

While it would have been possible to arrange the material in some other manner, the crucial debates concentrated on five major subjects: (1) the issue of original intent, (2) the question of precedent, (3) liberty and the bill of rights, (4) privacy, and (5) equal protection. Several other issues, such as Bork's role in Watergate, consumed a great deal of the committee's time but seemed irrelevant to the purpose of this book. In addition, much of the debate over free speech became pointless in light of subsequent comments by Bork during the hearing. The essential points of disagreement have been captured in the edited dialogue included herein.

CHAPTER ONE

BORK'S OPENING STATEMENT

At age 60 Robert Bork had behind him an outstanding career, with strong credentials both in academic and legal circles. Among all the Supreme Court nominees in recent years, as former Chief Justice Burger noted, there was no one with better qualifications than Bork.

Bork moved intellectually through socialism and a brief curiosity about communism during his high school and undergraduate years, into libertarianism, finally adopting the conservative views he had held for some time. He had been greatly influenced by conservative instructors at the University of Chicago, where he earned both undergraduate and legal degrees.

After law school he entered private practice, first in New York, then in Chicago. His specialty was antitrust, and his 1978 book, *The Antitrust Paradox*, would be an oft-cited work during the course of the hearings.

In 1962 Bork accepted a teaching post at Yale Law School. There he was a colleague of Alexander Bickel, former law clerk to Justice Felix Frankfurter and an authority on the Fourteenth Amendment. They would team-teach a seminar in constitutional law, an academic experience that would have great influence in developing Bork's own constitutional theory.

Tapped by Nixon for the office of Solicitor General in 1973, he became involved in the Watergate controversy when, on the order of the President, he fired special prosecutor Archibald Cox. That event, not discussed below since it had little bearing on the constitutional questions examined here, would be an important concern to Bork's opponents at the hearings.

He returned to Yale in 1977, where he held two distinguished chairs, but with the advent of the Reagan administration and the opportunity for a high judicial position, he left Yale. Bork went into private practice in Washington. He was appointed to the D. C. Circuit in 1982, and it was while in that judgeship that Reagan chose him to replace Powell.

Bork's scholarly writings, in addition to his antitrust book, included two major articles about which he was frequently questioned by the committee. One was a 1971 article, "Neutral Principles and Some First Amendment Problems," in the *Indiana Law Review*. His December 1968 Fortune magazine article, "The Supreme Court Needs a New Philosophy," received almost as much attention.

Popular on the lecture circuit, he spoke frequently before conservative audiences, delivering speeches that would be singled out for close scrutiny in the anti-Bork campaign waged by various civil rights, women's, and minority groups during the weeks prior to, and during, the hearings. Much of the questioning by the Judiciary Committee would focus on those writings and speeches as the Senators tried to determine if he still held those views and, more importantly, whether they would influence his decisions on the Court.

THE STATEMENT

I want to begin by thanking the President for placing my name in nomination for this most important position. I am flattered and humbled to have been selected. If confirmed, I assure the Senate that I will approach the enormous task energetically and enthusiastically and will endeavor to the best of my ability to live up to the confidence placed in me.

I also want to thank President Ford and Senators Dole and Danforth and Congressman Fish for their warm remarks in introducing me to the Senate and to this committee. This is in large measure a discussion of judicial philosophy, and I want to make a few remarks at the outset on that subject of central interest.

That is, my understanding of how a judge should go about his or her work. That may also be described as my philosophy of the role of a judge in a constitutional democracy.

The judge's authority derives entirely from the fact that he is applying the law and not his personal values. That is why the American public accepts the decisions of its courts, accepts even decisions that nullify the laws a majority of the electorate or of their representatives voted for.

How should a judge go about finding the law? The only legitimate way, in my opinion, is by attempting to discern what those who made the law intended. The intentions of the lawmakers govern, whether the lawmakers are the Congress of the United States enacting a statute or whether they are those who ratified our Constitution and its various amendments.

Where the words are precise and the facts simple, that is a relatively easy task. Where the words are general, as is the case with some of the most profound protections of our liberties — in the Bill of Rights and in the Civil War Amendments — the task is far more complex. It is to find the principle or value that was intended to be protected and to see that it is protected.

As I wrote in an opinion for our court, the judge's responsibility "is to discern how the framers' values, defined in the context of the world they knew, apply in the world we know."

If a judge abandons intention as his guide, there is no law available to him and he begins to legislate a social agenda for the American people. That goes well beyond his legitimate power.

To state that another way, the judge must speak with the authority of the past and yet accommodate that past to the present.

The past, however, includes not only the intentions of those who first made the law, it also includes those past judges who interpreted it and applied it in prior cases. That is why a judge must have great respect for precedent. It is one thing as a legal theorist to criticize the reasoning of a prior decision, even to criticize it severely, as I have done. It is another and more serious thing altogether for a judge to ignore or overturn a prior decision. That requires much careful thought.

Times come, of course, when even a venerable precedent can and should be overruled. The primary example of a proper overruling is *Brown v. Board of Education*, the case which outlawed racial segregation accomplished by government action. Brown overturned the rule of separate but equal laid down 58 years before in *Plessy v. Ferguson*. Yet Brown, delivered with the authority of a unanimous Court, was clearly correct and represents perhaps the greatest moral achievement of our constitutional law.

Nevertheless, overruling should be done sparingly and cautiously. Respect for precedent is a part of the great tradition of our law, just as is fidelity to the intent of those who ratified the Constitution and enacted our statutes. That does not mean that constitutional law is static. It will evolve as judges modify doctrine to meet new circumstances and new technologies. Thus, today we apply the First Amendment's guarantee of the freedom of the press to radio and television, and we apply to electronic surveillance the Fourth Amendment's guarantee of privacy for the individual against unreasonable searches of his or her home.

I can put the matter no better than I did in an opinion of my present court. Speaking of the judge's duty, I wrote: "The important thing, the ultimate consideration, is the constitutional freedom that is given into our keeping. A judge who refuses to see new threats to an established constitutional value and hence provides a crabbed interpretation that robs a provision of its full, fair and reasonable meaning, fails in his judicial duty. That duty, I repeat, is to ensure that the powers and freedoms the framers specified are made effective in today's circumstances."

But I should add to that passage that when a judge goes beyond this and reads entirely new values into the Constitution, values the framers and the ratifiers did not put there, he deprives the people of their liberty. That liberty, which the Constitution clearly envisions, is the liberty of the people to set their own social agenda through the processes of democracy.

Conservative judges frustrated that process in the mid-1930s by using the concept they had invented, the Fourteenth Amendment's supposed guarantee of a liberty of contract, to strike down laws designed to protect workers and labor unions. That was wrong then and it would be wrong now.

My philosophy of judging is neither liberal nor conservative. It is simply a philosophy of judging which gives the Constitution a full and fair interpretation but, where the Constitution is silent, leaves the policy struggles to the Congress, the President, the legislatures and executives of the 50 States, and to the American people.

I welcome this opportunity to come before the committee and answer whatever questions the members may have. I am quite willing to discuss with you my judicial philosophy and the approach I take to deciding cases. I cannot, of course, commit myself as to how I might vote on any particular case and I know you would not wish me to do that.

I note in closing, though it has been mentioned by President Ford, that I have been fortunate to have a rich variety of experience in my professional career in the major areas of private practice, the academic world, government experience, and the judiciary. I have been an associate junior partner and senior partner in one of the nation's major law firms. I have been a professor at the Yale Law School, holding two named chairs, as Chancellor Kent Professor, once held by William Howard Taft, and as the first Alexander M. Bickel Professor of Public Law.

For almost four years I served as Solicitor General of the United States, in which capacity I submitted hundreds of briefs and personally argued about 35 cases before the Supreme Court of the United States.

Finally, for the past five and a half years I have been a judge in the U.S. Court of Appeals for the District of Columbia Circuit, where I have written, according to my count, about 150 opinions, and participated in over 400 decisions. I have a record in each of these areas of the law and it is for this committee and the Senate to judge that record.

I will be happy to answer the committee's questions.

CHAPTER TWO

ORIGINAL INTENT

While Bork's opponents focused on more emotional issues — sterilization, abortion, marital privacy and equal protection — his supporters emphasized his conservative attitude regarding the role of the judiciary in interpreting the Constitution. In a series of questions Hatch, Thurmond and Grassley drew forth from Bork the conservative views that had made him a highly qualified nominee from the standpoint of the Reagan administration. Their questions gave Bork an opportunity to attack the development of a liberal Court over the past half century. With the right questions from the three conservatives, Bork built his case for judicial restraint rather than judicial activism, adherence to original intent as opposed to sociological jurisprudence and the role of the Court as interpreter rather than lawmaker.

But it was easy to build a position in response to friendly questions from Senators who already shared his views. It was something else to convince the nation when confronted by penetrating questions from Specter, who approached the subject not as one who believed in the philosophy of Bork's critics but who genuinely sought explanations so that he could understand how the seemingly rigid principles that guided Bork could be reconciled with the changing needs of the nation.

The debate between Specter and Bork was a reminder that both liberals and conservatives claimed Felix Frankfurter and Benjamin Cardozo. For years liberals argued that the Constitution should be interpreted through sociological jurisprudence, i.e., that the Constitution should be read in light of society's requirements. While Bork denied this position, his own testimony was full of repeated references to his belief that the Constitution could keep up with the needs of the nation without violating the framers' values.

In the course of the debate references were made to several cases. *Finzer v. Barry* (1986) involved the free speech of religious protesters outside the Soviet embassy. *Ollman v. Evans and Novak* (1984) was a libel case concerning freedom of the press. Those two, along with *Barnes v. Kline*, in which Bork justified an expansion of presidential power, were decided by Bork's appellate court. Raoul Berger's *Government by Judiciary* (1977), cited by Specter, strongly advocates the concept of original intent and is a leading conservative text on the Fourteenth Amendment.

The Testimony

HATCH

In recent years we have heard a great deal of commentary about the problems of judicial activism. This seems to be one of the central core matters here. How would you define judicial activism?

BORK

I would define it as a judge reading into a statute or into the Constitution his personal policy preferences.

No human being can sit down with words in a statute, with history and the other evidence he uses, and not to some extent get his personal moral view into it, because each of us sees the world, understands facts, through a lens composed of our morality and our understanding.

But there is an enormous difference between a judge who self-consciously tries to keep his biases out and tries to be as impartial on the evidence as he can be and a judge who incorporates his idea of wise policy into the Constitution or into a statute. As a matter of fact, if you're familiar with the academic legal debate, most of those writing in the law schools these days seem to prefer the latter kind of a judge, one who does not confine himself to the historical principles of the Constitution.

HATCH

In other words, judicial activism is when judges make law rather than interpret the law?

BORK

That is a good shorthand description.

HATCH

This may occur as well when judges make a general statement of law and stretch it to cover instances beyond that which the authors really intended; is that right?

BORK

That is correct.

HATCH

And that's what you mean by original intent?

BORK

That's correct.

HATCH

And it doesn't just mean original intent of the Founding Fathers or the original meaning of what they meant; it means the original intent of Members of Congress who are elected to make these laws, is that right?

BORK

'lhat is correct.

HATCH

I realize that you have been long known as a most eloquent, consistent and brilliant exponent of the classic theory of judicial restraint. What is meant by judicial restraint?

BORK

I've never liked the word judicial activism. I prefer something else, be-cause a restrained judge should be active in defending those freedoms and powers that are actually in the Constitution — should give them liberal construction. But he should not go beyond that, and that is judicial restraint. It is the morality of the jurist who selfconsciously renounces power and tries to enforce the will of the lawmaker.

HATCH

When courts read into the Constitution or particular pieces of legislation policies and rights that are not there, what happens to the ability of the legislatures of the respective States or of the Congress itself to make laws according to the needs of the people?

BORK

The people and their representatives have suddenly been ousted from an area that was legitimately theirs and the courts begin to set a social agenda instead of the people setting their social agenda.

HATCH

Can judicial activism be employed just as easily to reach illegitimate conservative as well as illegitimate liberal results?

BORK

Up until the mid-1930s, a conservative majority on the Supreme Court was reading its economic preferences into the Constitution. Labor laws were struck down, laws protecting workers were struck down. That changed. I don't think activism is any more proper for a conservative than it is for a liberal. That's why I don't think my philosophy of judging has anything to do with liberalism or conservatism.

HEFLIN

In some of your writings you have used the term "judicial imperialism." You make a distinction between judicial activism and judicial imperialism. What is the distinction?

BORK

Activism does not mean the same thing as imperialism to me. Courts should be active in enforcing the Constitution and the statutes. I do not believe in a passive court that just sits there and defers to everybody. On the other hand, imperialism implies that somebody is taking over territory that does not belong to them. That is what I mean — when a court takes over a territory that belongs to the legislature.

THURMOND

Some have said that you are a conservative activist. My impression is that your writings and your opinions on the Court indicate that you are a strong proponent of judicial restraint.

Would you briefly explain to the committee what you believe is the role of a judge in interpreting the Constitution and the laws of this country?

BORK

I think the obligation is to do the will of the lawmaker. If the lawmaker is Congress, writing a statute, or the lawmakers are the ratifying conventions of the Constitution, you determine the will, the value, that was intended in a number of ways: from the text, which may not be all that clear sometimes; from the legislative history and the expectations and public discussions surrounding the enactment of the law or the Constitution; from the way people at the beginning interpreted it, people who could be expected to know more about it than we know now. In a variety of ways, you manage to define a principle that you can apply to modern circumstances.

GRASSLEY

There are many arguments advanced why judges ought to be able to make law. One is that judges are an "elite" of our society, better educated than the masses, best able to protect society from itself. A second argument often used is that judges have a duty to protect all those who are under-represented in the political process. May I have your analysis of these arguments about judicial imperialism?

BORK

The first argument is one that is very commonly made by those who do not believe in original intent but believe in a judge creating constitutional values by the method of moral philosophy. There are a lot of academics who believe that. The usual ground for that is that judges are better at matters of principle than legislators are; that legislators are better at matters of expediency than judges are.

GRASSLEY

Are any of these arguments persuasive enough in your mind to allow a judge to make law?

BORK

Absolutely not.

GRASSLEY

Do not legislatures do dumb things sometimes, and are not the courts sometimes the only institutions in a position to protect society from such laws?

BORK

I am bound to say, Senator, yes, they do dumb things sometimes. And often those dumb things are unconstitutional.

But if you say to me here is an outrageous statute, and that is all the lawyer can say to me, that is not enough for me to strike it down. It may be one of the worst statutes the world has ever seen, and you and I would agree that no civilized community could really live with a statute like that. But unless I as a judge, unelected, unrepresentative, have a warrant in the Constitution, fairly applied, fairly interpreted, I will not strike it down because I regard it as outrageous.

It is a regular form of rhetoric to say that, if you would say a statute is not unconstitutional, that must be because you like the statute. That is not right. The question is never whether you like the statute; the question is, is it in fact contrary to the principles of the Constitution.

SIMON

I had my staff dig out the *Dred Scott* decision and I read the majority opinion by Justice Taney. It sounded an awful lot like Robert Bork in terms of saying we cannot read into the Constitution what is not there, when they denied free blacks the right to be citizens.

BORK

Senator, I take that a little hard. That does not sound a lot like Robert Bork. The *Dred Scott* decision is the first time the doctrine of substantive due process was raised by the Court — substantive due process being the doctrine that the due process clause imposes limits on government, and the Court makes it up. It is one of these free-floating things which the Court used in the past to strike down economic regulation.

BIDEN

Substantive due process means, to make sure we all understand it, that a court is saying, liberty means the following. Or life means the following, pursuit of happiness. They are going in and making a value judgment.

BORK

Yes. The substantive due process approach has been severely criticized by Hugo Black, Felix Frankfurter and a number of justices on the Court because it is without guidance for judges.

BIDEN

As you well know, distinguished jurists like Harlan, Jackson, Cardozo, Frankfurter, Burger and Powell all at one time or another have used substantive due process.

BORK

While I do not like substantive due process, I would certainly as a judge do my utmost to see if there is a legitimate constitutional ground to uphold freedom. I think that is a judge's duty.

Chief Justice Taney in *Dred Scott* said that it would be a violation of the due process clause to take away a black slave from a white owner.

So you see, these doctrines which give judges power to make up their own constitutional law, which was what Taney did in that case, do not always produce results that today we think are fine. Sometimes they produce disastrous results. And *Dred Scott* produced a disastrous result not only for Dred Scott, but for the nation and helped to lead up to the Civil War.

SIMON

Let me just quote the Chief Justice at that point. "It is not the province of the Court to decide upon the justice or injustice of the policy or impolicy of these laws. The decision of that question belonged to the political or lawmaking power, those who formed the sovereignty and framed the Constitution. The duty of the Court is to interpret the instrument they have framed, with the best lights we can obtain on the subject, and to administer it as we find it according to its true intent and meaning when it was adopted."

BORK

Anybody — the Devil — can quote scripture, and Taney can talk about original intent, as people did. But the fact is he used the due process clause in a way he never should have used it, against the black man, and Curtis' dissent is the original intent position in that case.

SPECTER

That brings up the subject as to original intent and how firmly committed you are to accepting stare decisis. I am concerned about your views for two reasons.

One, the next case will have a shading and a nuance and I am concerned about your philosophy and your approach. Secondly, I am concerned about your acceptance of these cases. You have written and spoken, ostensibly as an original interpretationist, of the importance of not allowing the mistakes of the past to stand.

BORK

I have also said that the commerce clause and the federal power generally was probably not intended, but they have to stand because it is too late in the day to overturn them-too much has happened, too much has grown up around them: statutes, institutions, expectations, and so forth. I have said that about a number of areas.

I don't think a person who believes in original intent can do without a doctrine of precedent; otherwise, he would be constantly trying to rip up the nation and its laws, and you can't do that.

SPECTER

But you have made some very strong statements about changing precedents where they are at variance with original intent.

BORK

That certainly is one factor to be considered, no doubt about it.

But if a judge sits down and he cannot understand what the Constitution is driving at, he has no idea, then I do not know what he applies. And if his job is to interpret the law and not to make it, I do not know what he does. To those who say you cannot understand the Constitution, I think that is dead wrong. I think you can understand the Constitution.

SPECTER

Suppose you came to a point where you said that determining original intent is impossible. Would it follow, then, that you could not have judicial review in this country?

BORK

I think you would require a consensus of the people that they wanted judges to rule, even though the judges had no law.

SPECTER

There is pretty much that consensus by the tradition of our Court, isn't there?

BORK

I do not think so. The American people want judges to interpret the law, not to make it. I think that is pretty clear.

SPECTER

I agree with you about that. But the interpretation of the law does not depend upon an understanding of original intent.

BORK

You make a good point, Senator — but when I say original intent, what I mean is really original understanding, because law is a public act, and it is really what was understood generally at the time the Constitution was framed, not the subjective intentions of James Madison.

When I sit down and look at the Bill of Rights, and it says "freedom of the press," I may not know exactly what they mean, but right away I know what they are driving at. I know the central freedom, or the core of the freedom, that they are driving at. When they say "no unreasonable searches or seizures," not only from the language but from the history of the British and the way they behaved in this country with their searches and seizures and general warrants, I know what they are driving at.

So I do not think there is any difficulty in understanding the basic principles of the powers granted to Congress or of the freedoms preserved in the Bill of Rights and the Civil War Amendments.

SPECTER

This is a central theme, and I think there is some difference of opinion as to whether you can really find original intent, whether the tradition of U.S. constitutional interpretation looks to specific constitutional rights as, for example, privacy, or a more generalized context. Justices who advocate restraint, like Frankfurter, talk about values rooted in the conscience and tradition of the people. The history of U.S. constitutional jurisprudence has in many, many cases not been grounded on original intent. Sometimes, yes, but frequently not.

It would be my thought that as the Court goes forward, and if you are confirmed, that there would be more flexibility in the application of constitutional law. I look to your own writings on the question of whether you can really find original intent.

In 1968 in Fortune Magazine you set forth a theory of constitutional law. "The text of the Constitution, as anyone experienced with words might expect, is least precise where it is the most important. Like the Ten Commandments, the Constitution enshrines profound values, but necessarily omits the minor premises required to apply them."

From that statement, it seems to me that it is pretty hard to find intent of the framers.

Then you go on: "History can be of considerable help, but it tells much too little about the specific intentions of the men who framed, adopted and ratified the great clauses. The record is incomplete. The men involved often had vague or even conflicting intentions."

In the Indiana Law Review article you say: "The framers seemed to have no coherent theory of free speech." "The First Amendment, like the rest of the Bill of Rights, appears to have been a hastily-drafted document upon which little thought was extended."

"The framers of the First Amendment probably had no clear view of that proposition."

And in your later speeches, you discuss repetitively the question about it is really the ratifiers as opposed to the framers and the conflicting views.

Now, in that context, where I think you are exactly right in what you have written and said, because of the great difficulty of finding intent, how much validity is there in searching for original intent as a necessary prerequisite for a constitutional decision, without which the Court has no legitimacy?

BORK

There is a lot of difficulty. But unlike the Ten Commandments, the Constitution and the Bill of Rights are closer in history, and we have a lot of evidence about the Bill of Rights now.

The remarks I made in Indiana, which you have just quoted, I took from Leonard Levy's book on the First Amendment. That book is now about 30 years old. I think he has found further evidence, and other people have found further evidence since then.

In the case of the Constitution we cannot know the framers' specific intentions. And indeed, their specific intentions would not help us a great deal because our task is to apply their public understanding of what they were protecting to modern circumstances as to which they could have no specific intentions.

What a judge needs from the Constitution is a major premise — what is it he is supposed to protect — and then he has to protect it.

We have the text. For example, the First Amendment tells us that it deals with religion, no establishment, free exercise. Right away we know that we are in an area, so that we know it is not just a free-floating liberty. We know they are talking about not establishing religion, and they are talking about free exercise of religion.

Then they say Congress shall make no law abridging the freedom of speech or of the press. So I know now that I am talking about speech and press, and the freedom of those two. I am not talking about a generalized liberty.

Now, you want to flesh that out. For example, you have a lot of contemporary debate about what was going on — the Federalist Papers, the Anti-Federalist Papers, and many debates. In the case of the Bill of Rights, we are a little short on debates in Congress, but you have some contemporary discussion; you have actions by the early Congresses which show what they understood themselves to have proposed; and you have actions by the early courts, which show what they understood to have been done.

And then you have, in the case of the free speech clause, or the free press clause, episodes of early history, such as the passage of the Alien and Sedition Acts and the terrible controversy that raged around those, so that we now understand that the Alien and Sedition Acts were in fact unconstitutional statutes. In this way, we begin to get a principle whose contours are not clear-çut. That is granted. But at least we understand the basic freedom they wanted to preserve.

Judges who look for original understanding and look at the same evidence and think as hard as they can will, in the borderline cases, often come out differently. I do not mean to say that original understanding gives anybody a mechanical way to approach a problem. It does not. But it gives them a pretty firm starting point.

SPECTER

As you define it, it does not seem to me that original intent provides any more specificity than the Frankfurter definition or the Cardozo definition of rooted in the tradition and history of our society.

You talk about fundamental values — and you have written on surveillance and electronic surveillance, which the Founding Fathers could not have anticipated; similarly, they could not have anticipated birth control devices. You talk about the concept of privacy. It runs through the Constitution, in a number of amendments.

Why is the doctrine of original intent sacrosanct? You point out that their specific intent is not clear-cut. Does that really advance the definition of constitutional values more than Cardozo and the nature of the judicial process?

BORK

You are making a very powerful argument from a very strong tradition. What I am saying also comes from a very strong tradition in our constitutional law, going back to Joseph Story and the first Marshall Court. If the concept of ordered liberty, which Cardozo and others used, turned out to be a continuing tradition on the Supreme Court — and I do not know where it stands now — and if it had a defined category so that judges were not free to make law at will, then I would not have so much difficulty with it.

GRASSLEY

Does the application of the Fourth Amendment in the 20th century, covering illegal electronic surveillance, or the First Amendment covering the electronic media, tell us that your philosophy allows the Bill of Rights to evolve?

BORK

Yes, it does, Senator. I wrote extensively about that in the *Ollman* case, and I did so because I was challenged by the dissent, about how can these rules ever change. I wrote extensively in that case about how rules can evolve in order to protect the original value that the framers wanted to protect, as circumstances and technologies change around us.

GRASSLEY

Could you give me your general approach to the problem of applying the words of the Constitution to problems that the founders could not have foreseen?

BORK

You look at the founders and the ratifiers, and you look at the text of the Constitution, their words, what it was that was troubling them at the time, why they did this, and you look at the Federalist Papers and the Anti-Federalist Papers and so forth to get what the public understanding of the time was, of what the evil was they wished to avert, what the freedom was they wished to protect. Once you have that, that is your major premise. Then the judge has to supply the minor premise to make sure to ask whether that value, that freedom, is being threatened by some new development in the law or in society or in technology today. Then he makes the old freedom effective today in these new circumstances.

That is going to mean changing legal doctrine, evolving legal doctrine, in order to protect the original value or freedom that the framers and ratifiers of the Constitution wanted to protect.

GRASSLEY

But you have to contrast the evolution of rights in the Constitution with what you might call the wholesale creation of totally new rights?

BORK

That is right. The freedom to be protected by the judge is always the lawmakers' — in this case, the ratifiers of the Constitution — and not the judge's values.

SPECTER

When I look at the question of original intent, I think it is fine in some cases where you can find it, and if you can find it, you ought to apply it. But so much of the time you cannot find it, and you ought not be hidebound by it. Frankfurter is right when he talks about the contours of the law being reasonably specific and not really subjective. You do not have to have an articulation of privacy to find it as a fundamental right in the Constitution or to apply it if the facts of the case require it in accordance with the needs of the nation, which is your language.

BORK

Yes.

SPECTER

If you look beyond the issue of original intent to the issue of legislative intent, there is a very interesting comment by Justice Scalia in the case of *Edwards v. Aguilar*, where he is talking about legislative intent — "Discerning the subjective motivation of those enacting the statute is, to be honest, almost always an impossible task." Going on, he says:

"To look for the sole purpose of even a single legislator is probably to look for something that does not exist."

Legislative intent in the statutes is very much akin to original intent of the drafters or of the ratifiers, and I am sure that every one of my colleagues here today would agree that legislative intent is nebulous and really nonexistent as you try to carve it out for an entire body of 100 Senators or 435 congressmen.

To what extent can you really bottom your opinion on what the Congress intended?

BORK

In the statute, Senator. I do not think I did too badly at getting at what Congress is driving at.

SPECTER

How do you know?

BORK

Sometimes Congress will tell you if they do not think you got it right.

SPECTER

We say very little on those subjects. Our reply power, our timing, is almost nonexistent. You might get a call — well, we would not call you up, either —

BORK

I meant you might amend the statute so that we got it right.

SPECTER

You can ask Senator Byrd about how difficult it is to pass anything through the Congress in terms of responding when something occurs. We are very good at inaction. You cannot tell anything by what we do not do.

BORK

All right. I think Justice Scalia — and he is a friend of mine, so he will not take this amiss — was taking an easy target when he talked about subjective intent.

I cannot tell what the subjective intent of various people is, but I can tell, from what they wrote and said, what the general understanding was. In the case of the Constitution, we have a lot of historical records — the research into them is constantly being improved—to show what the public understanding of the Constitution was.

SPECTER

Moving to the issue of legislative intent in the antitrust field, in your book on antitrust you say this: "Congress as a whole is institutionally incapable of the sustained, rigorous and consistent thought that the fashioning of a rational antitrust policy requires."

BORK

No group the size of Congress could accomplish the task. Large bodies simply do not reason coherently together. There are just too many people to sit down and draft a detailed antitrust law according to the teachings of microeconomics.

SPECTER

If that is so, Judge, and you may be entirely right, where does that leave the courts on enforcing Congressional intent?

BORK

Where it leaves me is this. The antitrust laws are remarkable statutes and, as the Supreme Court has said, they have the generality of provisions of the Constitution. John Sherman, the Senator whose act the Sherman Act really was and who did most of the explanation of it, gave examples of things that were to be illegal. He said for the rest it was left to the courts to evolve, to protect competition from case to case as they understood the facts and the competition.

SPECTER

But in your writings you complain about searching for congressional intent, and you refer to one Congressman who wants to have small businesses and not conglomerates or concentration in order to avoid slum housing in big cities. With all due respect, you ridicule that sort of legislative objective, and you say that, given the vagaries of what Congress has intended or what some Congressmen have spoken about in the antitrust field, it is too vague for judicial enforcement.

BORK

I did say that, but I was making a somewhat different point. This goes back to the main theme of my view of judging. There are commentators in the field of antitrust who want courts, through the antitrust laws, to impose or implement multiple values, often having nothing to do with competition. Then they point to somebody who said in the legislative history of the Clayton Act, Section 7, that where you have big business you have more smog and a higher lung cancer rate, or something of that sort. I was ridiculing the idea that a judge should take that and start measuring smog and lung cancer rates to decide whether or not a merger was legal, because that is a complete delegation to the judge to make any social policy. What a judge can do is look at the words of the statute, which say competition and monopoly; promote one, avoid the other.

SPECTER

But if the Congress is giving you multiple values, and you say that they have nothing to do with competition, you are the judge. You are supposed to carry out, under your theory, the legislature's intent. This is Madisonian majoritarianism. Who are you to say that these multiple values are not worthwhile?

BORK

If you look at the legislative history, no Congressman ever says: "Preserve competition, but if there is a conflict between that and smog, or a conflict between that and something else, make a trade off between them. Let a little injury to competition occur in order to reduce smog." No Congressman ever says a thing like that.

What they do is say: "We are passing a statute to improve competition." Then everybody gets up and makes a talk about all the other good things it will do. But those are side effects, I think, of the statute to preserve competition, not independent values that a judge is supposed to weigh.

SPECTER

The thrust that I read from your writing in the antitrust field is a conclusion of not a very high dedication to carrying out the congressional intent which you have written about in other fields.

Let me refer you to the section on price discrimination. You start off here: "The genesis of the Robinson-Patman Act is an oft-told tale. Enacted in 1937, the statute was a child of the Depression, as was so much pernicious economic regulation." When you call an act "pernicious," does that mean it is unconstitutional?

BORK

No, not at all.

SPECTER

How do you enforce a pernicious act?

BORK

You have to enforce it. You may not like it, but you have got to enforce it.

SPECTER

Well, how do you do it on the curved lines? How do you do it on the complex factual issues which are presented to you where, as the finder of fact, you have the discretion to find the facts, and you could arguably find them in a variety of ways so that an appellate court would not reverse you?

Does it color your thinking to find set of facts A, so that you do not have to apply this pernicious law?

BORK

I do not know. I have never been a trial judge, and I hope not. If I were a trial judge, I would try to find the facts as best I could from the contentions of the parties. It should be said that the scholarly opinion on all sides of the antitrust issue is that the Robinson-Patman Act is a peculiarly pernicious statute.

I am not out there as a judge to make the economy wonderful. I am out there to follow Congress' intentions. And when Congress has delegated to a judge, to the courts, the task of deciding when competition is threatened and when it is not, you do the best you can.

On the other hand, if Congress says: "This thing threatens competition; strike it down," I have to do that, even if I do not think it threatens competition.

SPECTER

How do you do that when Congress as a whole is institutionally incapable of a sustained, rigorous and consistently thought out fashioning of a rational antitrust policy?

BORK

I was talking about whether Congress could write a detailed set of antitrust regulations which made economic sense, and that would require a debate of economists for about a year, and I do not think the Congress has the time and it has too many people to have that kind of a debate. But Congress is certainly capable of adopting the general principle of preserving competition and giving some illustrations of what they mean.

SPECTER

I do not disagree with your interpretation of antitrust law, and I do not intend to pursue it any further. The limited point that I seek to make here on antitrust laws is the difficulty of finding congressional intent and the wide range of judicial discretion which necessarily applies. The practical effect of a judge's role is to apply that discretion and not to be able to really find what legislators' intend, and to try and make some sense out of what a judge may conclude to be a pernicious law, and to try to make some sense out of conflicting statements in the Congressional Record. A judge's role is to really try to pull the whole picture together, and that is the tradition of the law, and I think appropriately so. I think your antitrust writings make a lot of sense, and I think that that is what judges have to do.

But I do think that as you apply that beyond the antitrust field, into other legislative lines and into constitutional lines, there is a broader, traditional role of the judge in applying values to the needs of the nation beyond what you can find in some specific intent.

Let's go to the equal protection clause, which I consider to be a very central matter.

As recently as June 10, 1987, you say: "The equal protection clause probably should have been kept to things like race and ethnicity," and in the Indiana Law Review you had written in stronger terms that the equal protection clause applied only to race.

If you work from the framers' intent, and you have said that the framers' intent covered only race, how do you justify covering ethnic distinctions? How do you justify the *Yick Wo* case in 1886 involving the man who had applied for a license to have a laundry and got turned down in San Francisco? The case goes to the Supreme Court and they say equal protection applies.

Now, if you're an originalist, and original intent governs, and original intent was only to cover race, which you say flatly in the Indiana Law Review, how can you apply equal protection to ethnics?

BORK

I take it that Chinese people are a racial classification.

SPECTER

You're not saying that that's within the intent of the equal protection clause passed after the Civil War. The Civil War didn't involve the Chinese.

BORK

No, it didn't. But the equal protection clause clearly covers whites.

SPECTER

Does it clearly cover whites under original intent?

BORK

I think it does.

SPECTER

Where does that come from?

BORK

From the statements of the people who were involved in drafting and ratifying it.

SPECTER

There was an intent by the drafters and ratifiers of the Fourteenth Amendment to give equal protection to whites?

BORK

Yes

SPECTER

Where?

BORK

I don't have the citation in front of me. Congressman Bingham talked about almost everything that it covered. But he is not the only one.

If you go to the ratifiers, there's a great deal of talk about various things. If one approaches the amendment by saying it applies to groups, and you have to decide which group is covered and which group is not covered, then I think you're going to have to say they were talking about race and perhaps, as Justice Rehnquist has said, race-like things, whatever those are.

The difficulty is that the text doesn't read that way. The fact is that the Supreme Court, for all of this century and perhaps before, has come up with a reasonable basis test so that they have applied the equal protection clause under that test to everything, even to economic distinctions. If you take the reasonable basis test seriously, which they have not always done when they called it a rationality standard, then the clause applies to the reasonableness of all distinctions between people and it applies to things well beyond race. That is settled doctrine and it's been going on for a long time now. It doesn't require you to say which groups are in and which groups are out.

SPECTER

But if you accept that, you're totally away from original intent, which was for blacks, as you wrote it, as a racial issue. It doesn't talk about women, it doesn't include illegitimates, it doesn't include indigents, it doesn't include a whole pile of equal protection clause cases.

Absent the equal protection clause, you would find no basis for striking a State law simply because it didn't have a reasonable basis on a public interest, a classification logically related to achieving a legitimate State interest.

BORK

I think the equal protection clause is the primary, if not the sole, way to approach those things. There is a settled line of Supreme Court precedent running back at least 90 years which adopts a reasonable basis test and applies the equal protection clause to all kinds of things.

SPECTER

No doubt about that. And the Court, in doing that, has departed totally from the original intent of the framers and the ratifiers. The framers and ratifiers did not have women in mind, did not have illegitimates in mind, did not have poor people in mind, did not have Mexicans in mind, did not have Chinese in mind. I think the Court is right, and I'm certainly not objecting to that interpretation of the equal protection clause. But I am trying to square that with your very forceful statement that you are going to carry out original intent.

BORK

I have also said that anybody who tries to follow original intent must also have a respect for precedent, because some things it's too late to change.

The application of the equal protection clause to all kinds of people other than racial groups is so settled, and so many expectations have grown up around that, so many segments of our population have internalized that kind of protection, so many institutions are built on it, that it's an interpretation that should not be overturned.

The original intent philosophy I have been publishing for 16 years, and I don't intend to move from it.

SPECTER

How can you say that you're standing by original intent when you say that you're prepared to accept the Supreme Court decisions on equal protection which have deviated totally from original intent?

BORK

I don't know that that's entirely true. I think they were thinking about race. But I think they may have also thought about reasonableness. I'm not sure. I'm not an expert on this.

SPECTER

Wait a minute. You have written flat out — and this isn't a matter of accepting a Supreme Court opinion; this is a scholarly work — that when the equal protection clause of the Fourteenth Amendment was adopted, the framers and the ratifiers had race in mind and race only.

Do you now think they had something else in mind?

BORK

I don't know. I do not know that history. There's been a lot of historical research since then and I'm not relying upon original intent. What I am relying upon is a mode of analysis that the Supreme Court instituted in the last century. It seems to me a little late for anybody to tear that up, even if it doesn't square with original intent.

THURMOND

Judge Bork, as you know, the Supreme Court's decision in *Brown v. Board of Education* is one of the landmark decisions of the century. You have said that you think *Brown* was correctly decided, and you have praised *Brown* as an example of the Court applying an old principle according to a new understanding of a social situation.

Does this conflict with your views on how constitutional law should be read?

BORK

No, I don't think it does.

I have seen some evidence that the likelihood that the amendment was intended to stop segregation is greater than I had originally thought. *Plessy v. Ferguson* and the segregation laws came afterwards, when the Supreme Court had changed and the legislatures had changed in the South. So as a matter of original intent, I am not at all sure that segregation was not intended to be eliminated.

But let me proceed on the assumption that separate but equal was intended by those who framed the Fourteenth Amendment. The rule they wrote was no individual shall be denied the equal protection of the law. They may have written that rule on the background assumption that you could get equal protection or equality with separation or segregation.

If they did, then by 1954 it had become abundantly clear that the background assumption was false. You cannot get equality with segregation. At that point the Court faced a choice: Does it enforce the rule — equal protection — or enforce the background assumption that the framers and ratifiers made? I think it is clear that you have to enforce the rule, the background assumption being false, and that leads directly to no segregation, and it leads to *Brown*.

SPECTER

It seems to me, in reading the history of *Plessy* and the adoption of the equal protection clause of the Fourteenth Amendment, and reading Raoul Berger, that there was no question that the framers, or ratifiers, did not intend, in the remotest way, to cover desegregation. They expected to have segregated schools.

There were many States which had segregation. Five border States, eight Northern States. The District of Columbia schools were segregated. The Senate gallery was segregated.

The interpretation which you have advanced, that "separate but equal," in the absence of equality through separation, must lead to integration, seems to me to be at very sharp variance with what the framers had intended.

If you take a consistent interpretation, you cannot come to the result that the Supreme Court did in *Brown*.

But even on more fundamental grounds, you could not come to the conclusion that the schools had to be integrated on due process grounds. You have been very critical of the due process clause, saying that if there is not a specifically articulated right in the Constitution, you cannot derive it from due process.

But the D.C. schools were desegregated. Where can you find in the Constitution, in the due process clause, authority for desegregation?

BORK

Bolling v. Sharpe was the companion case to *Brown* and the Supreme Court there faced a problem because the equal protection clause through which *Brown* moved to accomplish desegregation applies only to States and not to the federal government.

You had the problem of the District of Columbia, and the only available constitutional clause, they thought, was the due process clause, which does apply to the federal government.

SPECTER

But the underlying question is why does the Court come to that position? It seems to me that it goes back to a statement you made that sooner or later the commerce clause would be interpreted in accordance with the needs of the nation, which is a very broad articulation of what the Supreme Court does, meeting the needs of the nation.

That certainly is not specified in the Constitution and is at variance with what the commerce clause says. If you read the history of the equal protection clause and the due process clause, and the status of segregation, you find that very much opposed to integration.

When you were asked which was the most controversial case besides *Griswold* you picked *Brown*. I think it was controversial because there was no legal underpinning for it.

BORK

Senator, I think there was. I have never read the briefs but I know some folks who have in *Brown*, and it begins to look as if there is historical argument that the framers of the Fourteenth Amendment did not like segregation and may have intended to do away with it. The black codes and segregation did not begin to come into the South until the Northern troops left the South. Later the Supreme Court changed. *Plessy*, after all, is a 1896 case, which is fairly long after the Fourteenth Amendment, *Plessy* being the case that said separate but equal is all right. That historical evidence casts some doubt on the flat assumption that the Fourteenth Amendment really meant separate but equal.

They wrote a clause that does not say anything about separation. They wrote a clause that says "equal protection of the laws."

I think it may well be true that they had an assumption, which they did not enact, that equality could be achieved with separation. Over the years it became clear that the assumption would not be borne out in reality, ever. Separation would never produce equality.

When the background assumption proved false, it was entirely proper for the court to say "we will carry out the rule they wrote" and if they would have been a little surprised that it worked out this way, that is too bad. That is the rule they wrote and they assumed something that is not true.

In that way I do not think any damage is done. You can even look at it more severely. Suppose they had written a clause that said "we want equality and that can be achieved by separation and we want that too."

By 1954 it was perfectly apparent that you could not have both equality and separation. Now the court has to violate one aspect or the other of that clause, as I have framed it hypothetically. The way the amendment was written, it was natural to choose the equality segment, and the court did so. It was proper constitutional law, and we are all better off for it.

SPECTER

I think we are better off for it too, but I do not think that that is a logical conclusion if you are looking at the framers' intent. But if you turn

to due process and take your application of due process of law and what
you have said about *Griswold* and *Roe v. Wade*, how can you justify *Bolling* applying the due process clause to stopping segregation?

BORK

I do not know that anybody ever has. That has been a case that has left
people puzzled, and I have been told that some Justices on the Supreme
Court felt very queasy afterwards about *Bolling*.

SPECTER

If you take Raoul Berger's analysis they felt very queasy about *Brown*
and *Bolling* because they came to a decision, essentially as you said it, in
accordance with the needs of the nation.

What I want to come back to is how that applies in other contexts,
how that applies in privacy, how that applies in equal protection. If you
are willing, as a Supreme Court nominee, to say that you sanction *Brown*
and you sanctioned *Bolling* on due process grounds, then it seems to me
you are a significant distance from original intent.

BORK

I do not think I am on *Brown*.

SPECTER

How about *Bolling*?

BORK

There may be a significant difference there, and I did not say I sanctioned it. I think that constitutionally that is a troublesome case.

It has been suggested that if the Supreme Court had struck down
segregation in all of the States under the equal protection clause,
Congress most certainly would have stopped segregation in the Dis-

trict of Columbia. It would have been a national scandal if they had not.

Bolling seems to have been propelled by a feeling that if we are going to do this to all of the States, we cannot let the federal government do it. I understand that feeling.

SPECTER

But as a matter of principle and as a matter of exponent as you are of neutral principles, if you can apply the due process clause as they did in *Bolling* why not in *Griswold?*

BORK

If they apply the due process clause that way, I quite agree with you. Why not in *Griswold* and why not in all kinds of cases? You are off and running with substantive due process which I have long thought is a pernicious constitutional idea.

SPECTER

I think it is as you articulate it, but if you start to deal with the needs of the nation and you accept *Bolling* to strike down segregation in the District of Columbia, and you accept it in the commerce clause, what happens to your principle?

BORK

Senator, I did not accept it in *Bolling.* When I say I accept it in the commerce clause, I accept it because what has happened is irreversible. You do it by a principle of stare decisis, a principle of following precedent so that we do not try to tear up the nation in a vain attempt to take the commerce clause back to where it was in 1790. That is all you can do. There is simply no point in a judge running around trying to tear down the federal government in the code book.

SPECTER

Final question: Do you accept *Bolling* or not?

BORK

I have not thought of a rationale for it because I think you are quite right. If you say it is due process and we will do whatever is fair or good under due process, the court's powers are unlimited. That is the problem I have with that substantive due process.

HATCH

These allegations continue to say that the vigor with which you would enforce *Bolling* would be colored by your conviction that *Bolling* itself is bad law.

Would your enforcement be hindered by an academic concern about the way that decision was reached?

BORK

No. A lot of people have had concerns about the way that decision was reached, but it is firmly in place. A lot of expectations, a lot of institutions and so forth have grown up around it. The due process clause has now been repeatedly used as if it had an equal protection component in it. I have no desire and I would not attempt either to overrule *Bolling* or to get the equal protection component out of the due process clause. That is established law.

SPECTER

I want to turn now to a statement you made in *Barnes v. Kline*. In your enumeration of the powers of the President, you said in your dissent that the Constitution "was to allow room for the evolution of the powers of various offices and branches, that the Constitution's specification of those powers was made somewhat vague. The framers contemplated organic development, not a structure made rigid at the outset by rapid judicial definition of the entire subject as if from a blueprint."

There, obviously, you treat executive powers as a blueprint in the Constitution with a fuller statement to be developed as organic law.

Why not such a similar interpretation for the Bill of Rights? Why the necessity to find a specific constitutional right as a prerequisite for dealing with State legislative action?

BORK

For this reason. In the *Ollman* case I found a column protected by the First Amendment. As I explained there, there will be an evolution of the Bill of Rights as new threats to the freedoms guaranteed develop — whether those threats are developments in legal doctrine, as in libel law, or threats coming from technology, or whatever. You do have an organic growth. There is a lot of freedom in that. These are questions of degree and questions of judgment, which is why you need judges and not just read the Constitution.

But I do not think that I can ever justify a judge putting a freedom or value in the Constitution that the framers or the ratifiers in no way contemplated. They did not contemplate the circumstances, so you may get an evolution for that reason. They did not contemplate future developments, so you may get an evolution of a value that is in the Constitution. But I think they have to put the value there.

SPECTER

But in *Barnes*, when it comes to executive power you allow for growth. In your opinion in *Ollman v. Evans and Novak*, where Judge — now Justice — Scalia criticized you as going beyond the intent of the framers, you did expand the constitutional right, and your opinion in *Ollman* might be said to have some similarities to Justice Douglas' opinion in *Griswold*. That is an articulation by a judge of a constitutional right which at least

Justice Scalia said was not within the intent of the framers.

Why not that as a general principle of constitutional law?

BORK

In *Ollman* I had a constitutional freedom specified in the Constitution, and the question was what it takes to protect that freedom, and
I evolved that. Justice Douglas did not point to any freedom or value
specified in the Constitution, and I think that is the difference between
the two cases.

SPECTER

Liberty is in the Preamble of the Constitution. You have objected to
an interpretation or a specification of liberty rights in your writings on
Meyer v. Nebraska and *Pierce v. Society of Sisters*, but why not liberty in the
very Preamble of the Constitution as a basis for privacy in *Griswold?*

BORK

You can use liberty in the Fourteenth Amendment. It speaks of no person may be deprived of life, limb, or liberty without due process of law.

SPECTER

Well, I do not pick that one up because it is due process, which you have
objected to. That is why I picked the fundamental of liberty from the
preamble. But take liberty either place. It is a cherished value; it is the
cornerstone of the Constitution. It seems to me as rational to say that
privacy is derived from liberty, that liberty implies privacy, as it does to
say that freedom of the press implies the Evans-Novak rights which you
found in the *Ollman* case.

BORK

The difficulty is that if I decide that I am going to protect liberty in general, without any specific provisions of the Constitution, then obviously I cannot say everybody is free to do whatever they want to do, and no statute may exist because it interferes with liberty. We cannot have anarchy. So then I have to define what liberties — without guidance from the Constitution — people ought to have and what liberties they ought not to have.

That is exactly the effort I engaged in for about six or seven years in a course on constitutional theory that I taught with Alex Bikel. I became convinced that it was an utterly subjective enterprise and that I was running my values into what I was coming up with. Each of us may have a different idea about what liberty requires. If we have no guidance from the Constitution itself, it is just the judge legislating the Constitution. If a judge said, "I think I will enact a statute," we would all recognize that that was improper. But a statute, I assume, Congress could repeal. If a judge legislates the Constitution, the situation is far more serious, and I do not want judges, including me, going around, saying, "You have this liberty, you do not have that liberty," and I cannot explain why I got it.

SPECTER

But why should you be free to find additional executive powers, as you say you can in *Barnes*, moving from a blueprint?

You said the Constitution's specification of those powers was made somewhat vague, that the framers contemplated organic development. Why not organic development for liberty? Why only organic development for executive power?

BORK

But it is not only executive power. It is also congressional power. There has been an organic development of congressional power, too, in this country.

SPECTER

All right. This really focused on executive power. But take it as you have articulated it. Why organic development for congressional or executive power? Why not organic development for people power, defined as liberty?

BORK

There is one decisive difference between you and me, Senator Specter, and that is you were elected. I was not. If the people do not like what you are doing with respect to liberty, they have a cure. If they do not like what I am doing with respect to liberty, they have no recourse.

SPECTER

You were not elected when you decided the *Ollman* case.

BORK

That is right. But I had a constitutional provision, a constitutional liberty, specified for me, and I was empowered to do my best to ask what is required in this case to protect that freedom.

I do not mean to say that judges do not have latitude, and they may not decide different things differently. But at least I knew that I had a constitutional liberty with a lot of Supreme Court decisions about how broad that liberty was supposed to be. But I could not go off and say I will take the First Amendment and decide a case about minimum wage laws.

We should remind ourselves that there was a time when the word "liberty" in the Fourteenth Amendment was used by judges to strike down social reform legislation. They struck down, in the *Lochner* case, law regulating the hours that bakers could work. They went through social reform laws very fast, in the name of liberty, and struck them down. I cannot say they are right or wrong about liberty. I can say they were wrong because they were using a concept to reach results they liked, and the concept did not confine them, and they should not have been using that concept.

DECONCINI

I want to turn your attention to *Finzer v. Barry.* I want to acknowledge that the Supreme Court has granted certiorari in the case, and that it would be improper for you to comment on any aspect of the issues presented by that case, so I am not going to try to do that.

The question that I do have is how do you determine the framers' intent, and is that activism as you explain that?

In that opinion you state:

"The framers understood that the protection to foreign embassies from insult was one of the central obligations of the law of nations. It is also clear that the Founders who explicitly gave Congress the power to enforce adherence to the standards of the law of nations, which they understood well, saw no incompatibility between the national interest and any guaranteed individual freedom."

I find this to be an interesting quote. When a decision, in your opinion, calls for an analysis of the framers' intent, I want to know how you come to that.

In this particular decision you did a thorough and long overview of threats to embassies and how governments attempted to protect them. You cited "Blackstone's Commentaries," a letter written by Millard Fillmore in 1851, an article written on the law of the nations in 1863, an incident in Philadelphia in 1902 in which a foreign flag was burned and no one was prosecuted, a U. S. Attorney General's opinion in 1794 that says the law of libel is strengthened in the case of foreign ministers because the law of nations secures a minister from insult, and a 1779 resolution by the Continental Congress urging that the right of ambassadors be protected.

This process seems to me a very laborious process that you went through. I enjoyed reading it for the history involved in it. When you are a non-activist and a strict interpretationist, if you want to call it that, or believe in the original intent that we have discussed here, how do you rationalize this long historical basis for your decisions that seems to go far away from the original intent?

BORK

I am trying to understand why you think I departed from the original intent, because I thought that is what I was talking about, for the most part.

Let me say one thing about activism and result orientation. "Result orientation" is a term of art describing some judges methods for judging a case, in which a judge would pay more attention to results than legitimate reasoning.

The people in this case who brought the lawsuit and whom I ruled against were conservatives who wanted to go out and speak, pray, and congregate in front of the Soviet and the Nicaraguan embassies. When I ruled against them, it was not exactly an action of a conservative activist.

This Congress passed the statute and the only question was is it constitutional. It prevents people from carrying placards, as I recall, offensive to a foreign embassy within 500 feet, or congregating there. It has therefore both aspects. One is the aspect of protecting the security of the embassy. We had affidavits about the difficulty. If we allow people right up close it becomes almost impossible for the police to protect the security of the embassy and the aspect of insult to the ambassador and his staff. That is what Congress had in mind.

Those are deeply-rooted in our constitutional tradition. The framers were worried about insult to ambassadors. The Continental Congress was worried about it. In fact, one reason for a Constitutional Convention was that before the Constitution they had to rely upon the States to protect ambassadors, and not all the States would do so, and our foreign relations were in kind of a tangle and a mess.

Therefore in Article I, section 8, clause 10, Congress is explicitly given the power to define and punish offenses against the law of nations.

DECONCINI

My concern is that in your original intent as I understand it, you look to the circumstances when the amendment was passed, the intent of the framers, and I am concerned that here you looked at a letter written by Millard Fillmore in 1851, which is certainly not the time of the amendment, an article written on the law of the nations in 1863; an incident in Philadelphia in 1902. What troubles me here is that if you are truly what you say you are and what I believe you are, more an original intentor than an expansionist, how do you rationalize using this sort of thing to come to original intent? I just do not follow it. You do go back here to the Continental Congress. That certainly was in the time when this was coming about, 1779. But these others, really, I just could not figure out.

BORK

I went through all this history about the Continental Congress, about the old writers, like Batelle on the law of nations, and a complaint by the British government in 1794 because of a riotous assembly before the house of a foreign council, and the opinion of the Attorney General in 1794, and so forth. I first established that Edmund Randolph and John Jay and all these people had these views. John Jay subsequently said: "It is of high importance to the peace of America that she observe the law of nations," and the safety and dignity of ambassadors is central to that.

I established that as a matter of original intent. Then, I thought it important to point out that this has been a continuing intellectual tradition in the law, right down to the present day.

DECONCINI

So you used more current history to substantiate that that original intent has been followed, is that what you are saying?

BORK

Yes. Chief Justice John Marshall, in *McCulloch v. Maryland*, not only cited the original meaning of the Constitution, but he brought the practice under the Constitution down to his day to show that that supported his understanding of the original intention.

DECONCINI

Okay, I understand it now.

GRASSLEY

I think you did a very good job of explaining to this committee the very important distinction between the result in a case and the reasoning behind that result. In other words, you may agree with the result as a policy matter, but still quarrel with the reasons supporting that result.

Can you explain to the committee why the reasoning of a court is often more important than the mere result?

BORK

A judge has power over people, and since he is unelected and probably unrepresentative of the American people, it is important that he demonstrate by his reasoning that there is law that he is applying and that he is not applying his personal values or principles. That is why the reasoning in an opinion is crucial. That is the judge's showing of his warrant to do what he does. That is the only thing a judge has to prove to the public that what he does in this case, and why this person loses, and why the rule is as it is, is a legitimate rule and a legitimate result. He must show his warrant by reasoning from the Constitution or from the statute.

Opinions serve a lot of functions. One, the losing party at least is given a good reason why he or she lost, and that is important, that people understand that they were heard, and that a reason has been given. It also is a statement to the public that the judge is exercising his or her power legitimately. It is also an essay, in a sense, to other people who may be affected in the future by this area of the law so that they can predict likely developments in the law.

Opinions serve a lot of functions.

CHAPTER THREE

PRECEDENT, JUDICIAL REVIEW, AND SEPARATION OF POWERS

Closely tied to the dispute over original intent was the fear that Bork might vote to reverse the liberal decisions of the pre-Reagan Court on equal protection, due process, the First Amendment and on other rights, such as privacy, not tied to a specific clause of the Constitution. As a result, one of the most provocative portions of the hearings dealt with Bork's commitment to precedent.

During the publicity campaign to build opposition to Bork, liberal critics warned that he would turn back the clock to separate but equal, would force women into back alleys for abortions, and would authorize police raids on the family bedroom. While the Senators did not ask Bork specifically if he would vote to overturn *Roe v.*

Wade, Griswold v. Connecticut and other crucial cases, they made it quite clear that this concerned them. They sought an answer by questioning the nominee regarding his willingness to accept settled law and the circumstances that might cause him to reverse one of those controversial decisions.

The senators were also concerned that Bork would support court stripping, advocated by some conservatives who wished to prevent liberal judges from barring conservative measures. Through this tactic jurisdiction could be withdrawn from the courts on specific subjects by act of Congress. Bork's opponents, and the undecided Specter, wanted to know if Bork would support that ploy to stop the Court from hindering attainment of a conservative agenda.

Bork believed a greater threat to the authority of the Court came from a 1966 decision by the Warren Court, *Katzenbach v. Morgan,* which involved a literacy test imposed as a voting qualification in New York. Though the Court had long ago held literacy tests to be valid, the 1965 Voting Rights Act had proscribed such tests if used in a racially discriminatory manner. The act was challenged as an unconstitutional intrusion by the federal government into state-run election procedures. The Court upheld the act, recognizing the right of Congress to redefine the meaning of the equal protection clause through the enforcement section of the Fourteenth Amendment. Bork viewed the Court's finding as an unconstitutional enlargement of the power of Congress.

Sen. Kennedy saw Bork's concept of separation of powers as a barrier to Congressional efforts to force the President to comply with legislative intent. Kennedy had sued (*Kennedy v. Sampson*) the General Services Administration to force that agency to publish as a valid act a bill that was passed just before Congress recessed during the 1970 Christmas holidays. The Senate had authorized its secretary to receive Presidential messages during the recess, believing that would force President

Richard Nixon to either formally veto the bill or allow it to become law without his signature. Instead, Nixon ignored the bill and treated it as a pocket veto.

Kennedy's suit raised a fundamental question: did a legislator have standing to sue the President in such a case? The U. S. Court of Appeals for the District of Columbia had ruled for Kennedy, but the Senator now wondered whether Bork agreed that Congress had standing (the legal right to sue) or would he deny Congress that right? If so, what could Congress do if the President refused to recognize, for example, the War Powers Act?

The debate on separation of powers turned to antitrust law, Bork's specialty. His critics saw him as inclined to ignore Congressional will on that subject. Metzenbaum wanted to know how an originalist could ignore direction from Congress and apply, instead, his own interpretation of antitrust law. The heated exchange between the Senator and Bork highlighted the debate on antitrust.

The Testimony

Precedent

BIDEN

In 1981 in testimony before the Congress, you said "there are dozens of cases" in which the Supreme Court made a wrong decision. This January, in remarks before the Federalist Society, you implied that you would have no problem in overruling decisions based on a philosophy or a rationale that you rejected.

BORK

Let me mention that Federalist Society talk. I had some notes, but I scribbled something in the margin which I got up and said in response to another speaker. It was that a nonoriginalist decision — by which I mean a decision which does not relate to a principle or value the ratifiers enacted in the Constitution — could be overruled.

If you look at the next paragraph of that talk, which was written out and not the extemporized part, it contradicts that statement. The very next paragraph states that the enormous expansion of Congress' power under the commerce clause of the Constitution, is settled, and it is simply too late to go back and reconsider that, even though it appears to be much broader than anything the framers or the ratifiers intended.

So there is, in fact, a recognition on my part that stare decisis, or the theory of precedent, is important. Anybody who believes in original intention as the means of interpreting the Constitution has to have a theory of precedent, because this nation has grown in ways that do not comport with the intentions of the people who wrote the Constitution — the commerce clause is one example — and it is simply too late to go back and tear that up.

I cite to you the *Legal Tender* cases. These are extreme examples admittedly. Scholarship suggests that the framers intended to prohibit paper money. Any judge who today thought he would go back to the original intent really ought to be accompanied by a guardian rather than be sitting on a bench.

BIDEN

Can you give us any other examples of the numerous decisions you have criticized that might fall in that category of being settled doctrine now and would cause such upheaval to change?

BORK

There have been Bill of Rights cases, freedom of the press cases. A whole industry is built up around an understanding of the freedom of the press. It is too late, even if one wanted to, to go back and tear up the communications industry of this country.

Shelley v. Kramer. Shelley was a case decided under the Fourteenth Amendment. The Fourteenth Amendment, as we all know, applies only when government acts, when government coerces and denies equal protection of the laws or due process.

That was a restrictive racial covenant case, and the Court held that when a State court enforced that contract, that was action by the government, and, hence, the Fourteenth Amendment applied to private action.

I have never been for racially restrictive covenants. I argued in the Supreme Court that racially discriminatory private contracts were covered by Section 1981, a famous post–Civil War enactment, and outlawed as such by that statute. That was *Runyon v. McCrary.*

The difficulty with *Shelley* was not that it struck down a racial covenant, which I would be delighted to see happen, but that it adopted a principle which, if generally adopted, would turn almost all private action into action to be judged by the Constitution.

Let me give you an example. If people at a dinner party get into a political argument, and the guest refuses to leave when asked to do so by the host, and finally the host calls the police to have the unwanted guest ejected, under *Shelley* that would become State action, and the guest could raise the First Amendment. His First Amendment rights would have been violated because a private person got sick of his political diatribe and asked him to leave and the police assisted him.

In that way, any contract action, any tort action, any kind of action can be turned into a constitutional case.

There have been some suggestions that my constitutional philosophy or my reasoning about these cases is in some sense eccentric. It is not in the least bit. All of these cases have been criticized. In fact, *Shelley* has never been applied again. It has had no generative force. It has not proved to be a precedent. As such, it is not a case to be reconsidered. It did what it did. It adopted a principle which the Court has never adopted again. And while I criticized the case at the time, it is not worth reconsidering.

SPECTER

It's too late to tear up the doctrine of privacy?

BORK

We will face that when we come to it, Senator.

SPECTER

We're facing all these other matters this afternoon.

BORK

But some things are absolutely settled in the law. The incorporation doctrine is; I have told you the commerce clause is. These are things of not only long standing but all kinds of things have grown up around them. Any judge understands that you don't tear those things up.

When you ask me about a current controversial issue, I cannot, and I should not, give you an answer.

THURMOND

Would you please comment on what criteria you think are important in deciding whether to re-examine past Supreme Court decisions?

BORK

I think precedent is important, and as I have explained, anybody with a philosophy of original intent requires a theory of precedent.

What would I look at? Well, I would be absolutely sure that the prior decision was incorrectly decided. That is necessary. If it is wrongly decided — and you have to give respect to your predecessors' judgment on these matters — the presumption against overruling remains, because it may be that there are private expectations built up on the basis of the prior decision. It may be that governmental and private institutions have grown up around that prior decision. There is a need for stability and continuity in the law. There is a need for predictability in legal doctrine.

It is important that the law not be considered as shifting every time the personnel of the Supreme Court changes.

BIDEN

To make sure I understand you. You say that when a court made a mistake on a constitutional principle, that a judge, if he believed it was a mistake, should come in and overrule it unless—

BORK

Unless private expectations have grown up around it, people have internalized the right; government institutions, private institutions have grown up in reliance upon it, and so forth.

THURMOND

In a recent interview you indicated that "The commerce power of the federal government had been expanded well beyond probably what the ratifiers intended. I think it had to expand beyond that as this nation grew and became more unified. But the change in the commerce clause is almost entirely a Supreme Court development." The question is, do you believe that this expansion by the Court was proper?

BORK

It was inevitable, let me put it that way. The nation needed a strong federal government with strong powers. For a time, justices of the Supreme Court objected to that. But the fact is, the appointment power meant that sooner or later the commerce clause was going to be interpreted in a way that met the needs of the nation. That seems to me to be just the way this nation grew. It seems to me an inevitable development.

GRASSLEY

I refer to a statement made by Justice Rehnquist when he appeared before this committee. I quote: "A precedent might not be that authoritative if it has stood for a shorter period of time or if it were the decision of a sharply divided court."

I want to know if you agree with that view?

BORK

Yes, in major part I do. I suppose the passage of time by itself is not important. The only reason it is important is that if expectations, institutions and laws have grown up around the decision in that passage of time. That certainly weighs in favor of not overruling the decision. In a very short period of time, obviously, things are unlikely to have occurred.

On the other hand, the Court tends to lose confidence if it starts overruling cases that it decided 6 months or 1 year ago just because the personnel is changed. It is a complex question of when to overrule. I know the factors I would consider, some of them. I have never read a theory of when to overrule and when not to overrule a precedent that had any firmness to it. People just discuss various factors.

GRASSLEY

I think you commented well on how long a precedent has stood. What about on the issue of how sharply divided the Court might be?

BORK

You mean the first time?

GRASSLEY

Yes, and commenting on what Justice Rehnquist said.

BORK

Well, I suppose that would have some weight. On the first point, *Plessy*, which allowed segregation, was 58 years old when it was overruled, and a lot of customs and institutions had grown up around segregation. So that is not a dispositive point. I guess *Plessy* was a sharply divided Court. I cannot recall right now.

I would think that a sharp division in the Court would lessen the weight of the precedent somewhat, but not dispositively.

GRASSLEY

What does the Tenth Amendment mean to you today?

BORK

That is unfortunately part of what I was discussing when I was discussing the fact that the commerce clause is expanded in ways that it is simply too late for a judge to go back and tear up. I think the framers and the ratifiers had a rather clear idea that these powers were limited and had kind of clear contours to them. Indeed, the government operated that way for a long while.

But the fact is, beginning with the Civil War up through the New Deal, the idea that those powers were limited and not really national in scope got lost. Now we are operating in a fashion in which the Tenth Amendment, I am sorry to say, has almost no practical significance, and I do not really see how it can much, given the way the nation has grown.

HEFLIN

Do you have any thoughts pertaining to how you would approach the issue of *Roe v. Wade* from a stare decisis basis?

BORK

I do not want to discuss stare decisis in the specific context of *Roe* because that is getting awfully close to how do the factors apply there and therefore, how would you decide. But I will be glad to discuss my general approach to stare decisis and the kinds of factors I would consider. I do not think I can discuss how they might apply in this instance, because that would be too close to committing myself to a particular vote later. I think it has to be, in the first place, clear that the prior decision was erroneous, not just shaky but really wrong in terms of constitutional theory, constitutional principle. But that is not sufficient to overrule.

A number of factors counsel against overruling. For example, the development of private expectations on the part of the citizenry. Is this an internalized belief and a right? The growth of institutions, governmental institutions, private institutions around a ruling.

The need for continuity and stability in the law, which is certainly always a factor to be weighted. The need for predictability in legal doctrine. I think the preservation of confidence in the Court by not saying that this crowd just does whatever they feel like as the personnel changes. And the respect due to the judgment of predecessors on a legal issue, if they have explained their judgment.

Against that is, is it wrong, and secondly, whether it is a dynamic force so that it continues to produce wrong and unfortunate decisions. I think that was one of the reasons the court in *Erie Railroad v. Tompkins* overruled *Swift v. Tyson* — a degenerative force, I think what somebody called dynamic potential. That is the kind of thing you would have to weigh and that is a very fact-based, a very particularistic consideration about whether this is the kind of case that goes one way or the other. I think the Court has got to work out a better theory of stare decisis than it has now articulated.

HEFLIN

Is it fair to say that number one, you think that the reasoning that brought about the decision of *Roe* is wrong? That the decision, based on that reasoning, was wrong? And that unless some general right of privacy is shown to you to come from the Constitution or unless you can find, in the Fourteenth Amendment or somewhere else, some limitation on anti-abortion statutes, then basically you would have to, under your thinking, look to the area of stare decisis in determining whether or not you think *Roe* ought to be reversed?

BORK

That is correct. I would have to ask myself what the presumption in favor of preserving a prior precedent meant in this case and whether it was overcome by other factors.

BIDEN

You said when you testified before this committee back in 1982 that "a judge ought not overturn prior decisions unless he thinks it is absolutely clear that the prior decision was wrong and perhaps pernicious."

You said in your response to questions from Senator Specter that the substantive due process clause, which is the place from where the general right of privacy has been derived, was "pernicious."

Based on your own standard about what you do when a case is pernicious, it seems to me that the entire line of privacy decisions would be in some jeopardy. It is through the right of privacy that the Supreme Court protected married couples in their decisions and found a "marital right to privacy."

It is through the right of privacy that the Court protected the right of a grandmother to live with her grandsons in spite of an ordinance saying that you had to be a nuclear family. It is through the right of privacy that the rights of a father to see his children have been protected. What has been protected are important and fundamental liberties that predate the Constitution. I have them because I exist, at least from my point of view.

I am trying to get a sense of your view that when a case is wrongly decided or pernicious then a Supreme Court Justice should overturn it and you are labeling the due process clause, and within it a right to privacy, as pernicious.

Putting them together, it seems to me that you are inclined intellectually to overrule these decisions or similar decisions that will come up. You might rule that the right does not exist.

Could you comment on that generally?

BORK

The clause of the Constitution to which you refer says that no person shall be deprived of life, liberty or property without due process of law.

It seems to me historically clear that that is a clause that protects procedures. You are entitled to fair procedures before you are deprived of anything. Its only substantive content is that it is used to incorporate most of the Bill of Rights, which originally applied only to the federal government, against State government, with which I have no quarrel.

But there is yet a third meaning which is that judges decide when they do not like a law that somehow due process has a substantive content other than incorporation by which they can make law.

I think the first use of substantive due process came in the *Dred Scott* decision, a case in which a black slave claimed that he had become free because he had entered into territory where the Missouri Compromise forbade slavery.

Chief Justice Taney ruled against the black slave. He said an act of Congress which deprives a citizen of the United States of his liberty or property — he is talking about the slave master — merely because he came himself or brought his property into a particular territory of the United States and had committed no offense against the laws, could hardly be dignified with the name of due process of law.

What Taney did was decide that an act of Congress forbidding slavery in certain territories was unconstitutional under the due process clause. I just want to point that out because that indicates that the due process clause, when it is used substantively, has every capacity to be pernicious.

When I said in my prior hearing that a case should not be overruled unless it was clearly wrong and perhaps pernicious, "pernicious" I meant there in the sense of capable of having dynamic force, generative force, that would produce new wrong decisions.

There are some cases that may have been decided on the wrong rationale but that rationale has never been extended anyplace else, and there is no particular point in overruling a case like that.

BIDEN

As I understand the law, a Supreme Court Justice is not bound as a matter of constitutional law to accept the precedent that has gone before if he or she has another reason or rationale to disregard it. I am not saying you do. I just want to establish the principle.

BORK

That is entirely true. Every Justice I have ever heard of and every legal scholar I have ever heard of says that the Supreme Court may overrule prior cases. But they all place limitations on that.

BIDEN

But a circuit court judge may not overrule constitutional principles stated by the Supreme Court. Is that correct?

BORK

That is also correct.

If there is an incorrect constitutional interpretation, the legislature cannot change it. The political forces of the nation are helpless unless they can amend the Constitution. If there is an incorrect interpretation of a statute, the legislature can correct it. That is why it has always been true that the doctrine of stare decisis or a doctrine of precedent has applied more severely in statutory fields than in the constitutional field.

BIDEN

Give us an example of each so we all know what you are talking about.

BORK

The court decided *Plessy*, establishing the rule of separate but equal for the races, in 1896.

BIDEN

That was constitutional versus statutory?

BORK

That was a constitutional decision. The Congress could do nothing about that. And the Court overruled it in *Brown*. Now, this is a standard view. Justice Brandeis says stare decisis is not a universal, inexorable command. In most matters, he says however, it is more important that the applicable rule of law be settled than that it be settled right.

BIDEN

I just want to make sure that I understand. When it is constitutional, precedent is more binding.

BORK

No, quite the contrary. The reason for the distinction given by Justice Brandeis, Justice Douglas, everybody who talks about it, is that if a court reads the Social Security Act incorrectly, if a court reads the Mann Act incorrectly, Congress can correct the court instantly. It can pass a statute saying we didn't mean that, do it this way. If a court misinterprets a fundamental profound provision of the Constitution, Congress cannot change it.

BIDEN

Like the *Griswold* case.

BORK

Right, like *Griswold*, like *Brown*, like any case you want to choose.

BIDEN

I'm with you.

BORK

Congress cannot change it. That means, as everybody has said, the Court should be more willing to rethink a constitutional decision because only the Court can correct the mistake, nobody else can.

BIDEN

None of us can pass a law changing *Shelley*, changing *Griswold*, changing *Katzenbach*, unless we pass a constitutional amendment, because there is a constitutional principle in there.

BORK

Yes.

Judicial Review and Court Stripping

HEFLIN

I have a question or two about court stripping. As you know, section 2 of Article III refers to the appellate jurisdiction of the Supreme Court and has the exceptions and regulations clause contained therein.

Would you set forth your views on whether or not, first, the Congress, by an act of Congress, can in effect strip the lower Federal courts of jurisdiction pertaining to a subject matter; and second, as to whether or not the Supreme Court can be stripped by an act of Congress of certain jurisdiction pertaining to such matters, For example, there have been efforts made in busing, prayer in school, and other things of this sort.

BORK

I think it is conventional wisdom, and it has been so held in some cases whose names I cannot now recall, that Congress, since it need not have created the inferior federal courts, may deprive them of jurisdiction if it wishes, in which case, constitutional cases would start in the State court systems.

It has been argued that the exceptions clause of Article III would allow Congress to take away jurisdiction from the Supreme Court in whole classes of cases. As I recall, attempts have been made to do that in the abortion area, in the school prayer area, and so forth.

I have always taken the position that the exceptions clause was not designed for that purpose, and therefore cannot be used for that purpose.

It seems to me that had the framers and the ratifiers wanted a mechanism to curb a Supreme Court that was doing things they did not like, and return power to the Congress instead of to the courts, they would have written a clause that did that.

In fact, if you take away the jurisdiction of the Supreme Court everything would go to the State court systems. I do not think you can get the constitutional cases out of the State court systems. I do not think you can deprive the State court systems of constitutional cases because the Constitution says that every State judge shall be bound by this Constitution.

There are two reasons, then, why the exceptions clause was not intended for use in this fashion. One is that it does not return power to the democratic legislatures. The other is that it spreads the decision of the issue out into 50 different court systems. Then it would have been 13 different court systems, but the principle is the same. That means the exceptions clause could not be used in the most important cases.

For example, if a challenge to a draft law were made, and Congress took away the jurisdiction of the Supreme Court to decide the constitutionality of a draft law, you would have 50 different systems deciding that. And you cannot have a system in which the draft is constitutional in Ohio and unconstitutional in Indiana, and so forth across the country.

All these reasons lead me to believe that that clause was never intended as a way of checking the Supreme Court when Congress thinks it has created an excess. So I think it is really a housekeeping clause, a clause to be used for making court jurisdiction more efficient, and making things run better — not a checking device.

HEFLIN

I suppose you are familiar with the 1869 case of *Ex Parte McCardle*, which in effect ruled a little bit different. It may have been circumstances, and there may be distinctions between it. But would you address how that case, looked at from stare decisis, has an influence or lack of influence on your opinion?

BORK

I think the Supreme Court had actually heard argument in the case when Congress removed its jurisdiction over that kind of habeas corpus. The Court held that it was without jurisdiction.

Later, I think the Court said that there were other writs of habeas corpus that could be used so that Congress had not effectively prevented the Court from hearing that kind of issue. It just took that particular case away.

So I do not really know where the matter lies as a matter of precedent or stare decisis. I think it is somewhat confused.

SPECTER

If it is thinkable that we could proceed in this country without judicial review, and it is impossible not to have a doctrine where judges rely upon original intent, do you think that we have to abandon judicial review?

BORK

Senator, there is simply no possibility of anybody abandoning judicial review at this stage in our history. It is an absolutely firmly-rooted tradition in our law. The First Congress that wrote the Judiciary Act of 1789 gave the Supreme Court jurisdiction when State courts ruled a federal statute unconstitutional under the Federal Constitution.

That pretty clearly indicates to me that the people who knew most about the Constitution — that is, the First Congress — intended judicial review, because they did not tell the Supreme Court that it had to reverse any State court judgment holding a Federal statute unconstitutional under the Federal Constitution, nor did they say that State courts could not review constitutionality.

I think judicial review was intended from the beginning, and for that reason alone, I would not abandon it.

When I said it is thinkable we need not have started with judicial review, all I meant by that is we have other democratic societies like England, France and so forth, which have a long history of freedom without judicial review. We have it. We are not going to give it up. Nobody is going to cut back on it.

People say that discerning anything called an original understanding of the Constitution is impossible. Well, if it is impossible to know what the Constitution means, then I do not know where judges get their power to override democratic decisions, because I have always thought that it is the judge's job to interpret the law and not to make it and if you cannot understand the Constitution — which I think is a ridiculous claim; I think you can understand the Constitution — but if you could not, then I do not know what would authorize a judge to make law.

SPECTER

If you find that it is impossible to find original intent, can you still have judicial review? Your speeches, at least, are pretty categorical in saying that if you do not have original intent, you cannot have judicial review.

You and I both agree that constitutional law in this country mandates judicial review.

BORK

Yes.

SPECTER

But in the context where a presidential candidate is talking about judicial review being inappropriate, unnecessary, and in the context of an Attorney General's speech last year which raises a suggestion, although not perfectly clear, that the Supreme Court may not be the last word, but the executive and the Congress have the authority to interpret the Constitution, and then you look to some of your speeches, where you say that in the absence of applying original intent, you cannot have judicial review — I just want to be sure that you stand firmly for judicial review whether or not you have a common understanding of original intent.

BORK

I stand firmly for judicial review. I have never questioned judicial review. I have always thought it was an important part of our culture and our tradition and our law. And in America, it is an important part of our freedom. Perhaps we require judicial review more than England and France did because we have a much more pluralistic society and many more minorities to take care of.

HATCH

You said in the *Katzenbach* case that if Congress can undertake its own interpretation of the Constitution by a mere majority vote, then the Constitution is not going to be the anchor holding our nation in place during political crises; is that right?

BORK

My views on *Katzenbach* have not changed. I do not think that the Congress of the United States can change the Constitution by statute.

HATCH

Let me ask you directly, so nobody has any question about it. Was your criticism of the *Katzenbach* case based on your approval of literacy tests?

BORK

Absolutely not. I have no view of literacy tests. I have never looked at how they operate. I know some of them are discriminatorily used, but if they are non-discriminatory, I have no view of how they operate and none of my criticisms of any of these cases implies agreement with the statute which was being discussed. None of them.

That is only for a result oriented judge, a judge who wants results. I do not care about that. I care about whether it comes out of the Constitution and whether it is reached by proper constitutional reasoning.

In 1803 Chief Justice John Marshall decided the case of *Marbury v. Madison* in which he for the first time gave an extensive rationale for the power of the judiciary to strike down statutes. Central to his reasoning was the fact that the Constitution would be meaningless if Congress could alter it by a mere statute.

Katzenbach is in direct conflict with that historic decision because it did allow Congress to alter a constitutional provision by statute.

Congress can participate in changing the Constitution, but it does so by proposing an amendment to the Constitution which must go to the States, not by passing a statute.

HATCH

It is interesting that we on this 200th anniversary bring up the venerable case of *Marbury v. Madison* because basically that established the principle of judicial review and if we go the route of the *Katzenbach* case the way you have discussed it, then it would become the principle of political review rather than judicial review.

BORK

That is right. It would be a revolution in our constitutional structure and would mean the Constitution effectively controls nothing that the Congress wants to do.

HATCH

Anytime Congress wants to overrule it, they can do it, basically, under the *Katzenbach* theory.

BORK

Katzenbach could be a disaster for minorities. We all assume that Congress will only use its powers to alter the Constitution in ways that we like. That is by no means true. One cannot be sure of that.

Separation of Powers: Congress v. the President on War Powers

GRASSLEY

We have heard a lot about the issue of standing to sue in the federal courts. Remembering the fact that I am not a lawyer, I would like to bring up a technical area that I want to explore with you in the doctrine of standing. Explain your views of this doctrine.

BORK

My views are almost identical with those of the Supreme Court. It is a separation of powers doctrine, and it is a doctrine that is essential to keep the courts from dominating society. As Lewis Powell has said, standing is about the proper and properly limited role of courts in a democratic society. Chief Justice Marshall said courts are there to decide controversies when an individual or an organization has been hurt. It has to be the individual who has standing and not the issue involved which gives standing. Otherwise, courts could just take on any issue they wanted to and practically run the government.

Standing is a way of making sure that people are really hurt, suffered some injury, before they come in to litigate some large constitutional question or statutory question that they would just like to litigate out of interest.

There are two aspects of standing. One is the Article III core of standing. The Court has said that part of standing being a separation of powers question is demanded by the Constitution. But there is an additional aspect of standing which is not demanded by the Constitution, but the courts have required as a prudential matter. Congress is free to give standing in the area where courts would deny it on prudential grounds, but not free to give standing where the court thinks that Article III denies standing.

KENNEDY

Moving to another area, I would like to ask you about congressional standing to bring law suits challenging abuses of the Constitution by the President.

Obviously, as in the case of the War Powers Act, Congress cannot run the executive branch, and we cannot take the President into court every time we disagree with a policy of the administration. But that is not the issue. In a few very important situations, members of Congress should have the right to resort to the courts to preserve the constitutional role of Congress. That is what we call the doctrine of congressional standing, the right of members of Congress to sue in the courts.

In a dissenting opinion in 1985, you said, and I quote: "We ought to renounce outright the whole notion of congressional standing." Then you went on to state in that opinion: "When Federal courts approach the brink of general supervision of Government, as they do here, the eventual outcome may even be more calamitous than the loss of judicial protection of our liberties."

Since you issued that opinion, have you expressed any different view?

BORK

No.

The doctrine of congressional standing is the theory that if the President does not enforce the law the way Congress thinks it intended the law to be enforced a Congressman may sue to get an injunction or a declaratory judgment against the President to make him do what the Congressman wants him to do.

That is an entirely novel constitutional doctrine which I think was never heard of before 1974 in the case you brought, *Kennedy v. Sampson*, and it is confined to the circuit court on which I sit. I do not think any other circuit has ever picked up that doctrine. So it is a constitutional novelty, and it is by no means settled. And the Supreme Court has not passed upon it.

The reason I am troubled by it is as follows. What it will lead to is domination of the Government by the judiciary. If a Congressman has something akin to a property interest or something in the law he passes, if it is not carried out properly, so that his official capacity is in some sense diminished, then I think the President has an equal interest in not being forced to do things he regards as improper or unconstitutional. Therefore, if Congressmen may sue the President because he is not doing something under the law they would like, then if the Congress overrides a presidential veto and the President thinks that cuts into his constitutional office too much, the President can sue the Congress.

I spent some time as Solicitor General trying to get a case on the legislative veto. I wanted to see whether that thing was constitutional. If I had understood the theory of congressional standing, which is really governmental standing, I could have stopped hunting for a case. I could just have had the President sue the Congress and get a declaration right away.

But if it is true of a President and Congress, it is also true of judges. If Congress passes a statute that I think cuts into my powers, I can go to the Supreme Court for a declaration of unconstitutionality. In fact, that happened. Two judges in the Northern District of Illinois were reversed by the seventh circuit, and the judges petitioned for certiorari to the Supreme Court on the grounds that the seventh circuit had done things to their office which were improper.

Everybody is going to be in the federal court defining their rights of office instantly. What is important to remember about congressional standing is it is not the only way you can get those issues before the Court. If the President does something that is not in accordance with the law, there is almost always a private individual who can sue and who can show injury, and he can then challenge the President's action, which is exactly what happened in the old pocket veto cases.

KENNEDY

Congressional standing may not always be appropriate, but it clearly is appropriate when the President unconstitutionally claims a duly enacted law is not a law at all. I think we are not opening the floodgates by giving Congress the power to go into court in a narrow range of cases where the President has abused his power and denied the rights of Congress under the Constitution. You say that the Congress cannot even raise the question in court because that sort of litigation would open up the doors to all sorts of other abuses. I believe that is just another example of your attempt to draw a bright line that just does not make any sense. Isn't it true that in an article in "The Wall Street Journal," in 1978, you stated that the War Powers Act was "probably unconstitutional, and certainly unworkable?"

Since then, have you expressed any different view about the War Powers Act?

BORK

That is a very complex act. I think the consultation requirements probably seem constitutional. The notice requirement seems constitutional. But that act contains a legislative veto which, at the time, I thought was probably unconstitutional, and the Supreme Court in the *Chadha* case has since said that it is unconstitutional.

So I do not think that mine was a bad prediction.

If I had to construe the statute I would construe it in order to save its constitutionality as any judge should. There is one other possible problem with the act. The major questions of war, or peace, or questions affecting that, are most certainly for the Congress. Only Congress can declare war.

In fact the Congress need not give the President a single soldier. There is no constitutional requirement that it do so.

But at the other end of the spectrum, tactical decisions in the field seem to me to be for the Commander in Chief, and, for example — to take the extreme case — I would have very much doubted that during the Battle of the Bulge, Congress could have ordered the President to surrender the airborne troops at Bastogne rather than continue the battle.

There is a vast spectrum between the ultimate strategic question of war or peace and tactical decisions in the field, and it may be that some constructions of the War Powers Act might get Congress into clearly tactical decisions, but I am not sure about that. I have not looked at that for a long time.

KENNEDY

In 1971, you suggested that it was unconstitutional for Congress to stop the President from invading Cambodia. We all agree that the President is the Commander in Chief, and the Congress cannot manage and should not manage military tactics. That was very clear during the hearings, and during the debate on the War Powers Act. We cannot run a war, but we ought to be able to stop a war. That is just common sense in a democracy, and the American people have learned, with good reason, to be skeptical of presidential wars.

We all know what happened in Vietnam, and the same concerns were there when President Reagan sent troops into Lebanon, and the American people are obviously concerned today in regard to our policy in Nicaragua as well as the Persian Gulf.

BORK

Senator, the question of war or peace is entirely for Congress. Only Congress can declare war.

As far as Vietnam is concerned, Congress could have cut off the funds and ended that war, whenever. That would have been entirely constitutional.

My only question was a question of tactics within a war.

The ultimate power in this society about war and peace is Congress. It can declare war. It can not only declare war, it can refuse spending.

SPECTER

Judge Bork, realistically, what has happened on that?

We really, in the Congress, do not have the power to declare war anymore, given the realities of international events today. When the President acts in Lebanon, in Grenada, in the Persian Gulf, the reality is that the day of Congress declaring war is gone.

On the spending issue, the reality again is that Congress lacks the power, because once the President has dispatched a fleet to the Persian Gulf, it is unthinkable and impossible for the Congress not to fund that operation.

If we do not have authority under the War Powers Act to require a certain Presidential response and then to say no to the President, where does the Congress in 1987 exercise its congressional authority to declare war?

BORK

Well, maybe you can do it under aspects of the War Powers Act. I see your point, Senator, and it is a good point. I do not mean to dispute it. I had thought it would be a little easier to tell the President, "You have two weeks to get those ships out of there," and after that, no more money may be spent.

SPECTER

Who is going to tell him?

Separation of Powers: Congress v. the Court on Antitrust

METZENBAUM

Let's talk about price fixing for a minute, because it is part of this whole issue. Tell me in language that the American people can understand, how you can argue that price fixing is going to help the consumer?

BORK

In the first place, I think it is essential to distinguish between price fixing among competitors, which is illegal per se, meaning that it cannot be justified on any grounds. I have agreed emphatically with that rule. I think if competitors fix prices they should be punished. They should be sued for treble damages. They should be criminally prosecuted. No doubt about it.

We know why people fix prices. They want to make fatter profits than they should get under competition. We now shift to the manufacturer who wants to set the minimum price at which his retailers can sell. In 1911 the *Dr. Miles* case examined the practice and said, we would not let the dealers fix the price themselves and therefore it follows that we should not let the manufacturer fix their price for them.

That argument does not follow. The manufacturer who is fixing the price of the dealers has no reason in this world to want to give them a fatter profit. What he wants them to do, usually, is to compete in a different way — compete by providing information, by providing selling services, by adding things to the product.

Those are not bad activities and if he could own those dealers himself he would probably sell at the price he fixed and add those services. It is merely a way of doing by contract what he could do if he owned them, and the purpose is to get these people to compete in other ways and not below a certain price.

That may be pro consumer or not. It can be viewed as pro consumer because the manufacturer is not getting any monopoly profit out of this. The manufacturer has no incentive to do that unless more consumers respond to the particular behavior of dealers that he encourages with that price limitation.

Let me give you an example from real life. There was a time when you could set resale prices on things like television and big appliances. And when you did that, a store like Marshall Fields in Chicago would carry the full line of the manufacturer's products so they could show you every one, and they would have a knowledgeable person there to explain the differences because it paid them to do that.

Then, when resale price maintenance became impossible, a discount store opened up, and prices dropped. But people would come in and shop at Marshall Fields, look at all the models and get all the information and explanation, write down the model number, and go over to the discount store and buy it. That is fine, except Marshall Fields stopped supplying the information, showing all the models and so forth. If the Congress disagrees with me, all they have to do is say, no resale price maintenance.

METZENBAUM

But the fact is that the Congress has repealed the anti-trust exemption for fair trade laws. We have cut off funding, led by a Republican member of the Senate. When the Justice Department wanted to go in with an amicus brief on a resale price maintenance case, we cut off the funding and resisted legislative changes in the law.

Congress does not want to change the law, but you are the one who apparently wants to change the law through the Supreme Court.

Judge, in this area your view is very troublesome. You are on the opposite side of where you usually are, because here Congress has passed this law, Congress indicates that they like it, and for a court to change it today would be a rejection of Congress' will. It would be the court making law.

What assurance can you give us that the antitrust laws will be enforced and consumers protected if you should become a member of the Supreme Court?

BORK

I can give you every assurance, but it will have to be according to my understanding of what the law means and what the economics meant.

THURMOND

As economics advance, ideas change. Isn't that correct, Judge Bork?

BORK

That is entirely correct. A desire that judges adopt the Sherman Act to evolving economic understanding appears in the legislative history of the Sherman Act, and also appears in the rule of reason, which is the basic rule of the Sherman Act, laid down by Chief Justice White in 1911 in the great cases involving Standard Oil and American Tobacco.

In the Sherman Act, which merely says that restraints of trade are illegal, the Congress rather clearly gave a mandate to the courts to evolve the rules that would protect competition. And Senator Sherman said as much. He said he was really aiming at three classes of cases: at price fixing between competitors, at monopolistic mergers, and at predatory conduct by a firm which prevented competitors from competing effectively.

Beyond that, he said, the courts will have to evolve the rules to protect consumers from time to time. In *Standard Oil* and *American Tobacco* Chief Justice White explicitly said that these statutes are aimed at practices which restrict output.

He said the statute is aimed at the elementary and indisputable concepts of the common law about hurting competition. And he built into the rule of reason, which he announced in that case, a mechanism for evolving the law as economic understanding progresses. That is quite clear in the legislative history of the Sherman Act. It is quite clear in the great rule of reason cases, *Standard Oil* and *American Tobacco*.

As economic understanding progresses the law just evolves.

METZENBAUM

Today we meet with an unprecedented wave of mergers. From your writings I get the impression that this greater concentration of power in large corporations does not disturb you.

It disturbs this Senator and I think it disturbs many people in this country. In fact, you have written that such trends are desirable and should be allowed to continue until there are only two companies.

I quote. "We are in an area of uncertainty when we ask whether mergers that would concentrate a market to only two firms of roughly equal size should be prohibited. My guess is they should not. And therefore, that mergers up to 60 or 70 percent of the market should be permitted."

From this I can only conclude that you would look favorably on a merger which left only two firms in the oil industry, or the airline industry, the food industry or any other industry. I think at one point you said that maybe there ought to be three, but it does not matter to me whether it is two or three.

The fact is, you would accept total concentration of economic power in just a couple of companies, maybe three, depending upon which day you were writing, and I an not questioning that point. But the point that bothers me is, competition is so vital to this free enterprise system, and if we were to follow your line of reasoning there will not be any competition in this country because two companies will not effectively compete against each other. It will be a laissez-faire approach where they will let each do their own thing.

I would like to get your views on that.

BORK

I was arguing what the evidence showed about competition in concentrated markets at that time. I do not know if there is additional evidence or not. The Congress' statutes have been most imprecise about the size of allowable mergers. Section 7 of the Clayton Act, which is the primary statute dealing with mergers, just says, stop it if it may tend towards a monopoly or to lessen competition. It does not say anything about what market share should be allowed.

If you look at the legislative history, you cannot find out what market share should be allowed. If Congress has an economic theory and says no fewer than 10, no fewer than 20 firms, that is fine. I will follow that law.

METZENBAUM

It is what Bork says that concerns me, not what Congress says. I am concerned about your position that two or three companies can control a market and that is acceptable in the free enterprise system.

BORK

I do not think two or three companies can control a market unless they conspire.

METZENBAUM

But they can buy up all of their competitors. That is what is happening in America today.

BORK

I think most of those are conglomerate mergers, which are a different problem than a horizontal merger.

But if you have three companies in a market and they are not in collusion, it seems to me that the evidence from various industries, some of which I cite in the book, suggests that you get hard competition. If they conspire, you do not.

I do not think section 7 of the Clayton Act is going to allow me, even if I still believe that after I hear more evidence, to say, get down to three.

METZENBAUM

The fact is, you have six major oil companies in the world today and you have a lot of competition besides. But give a one-cent or two-cent increase in gasoline and they all go up at the same time, and that is just a given.

With three companies and no competition beyond that, or two companies, as you have written, I frankly feel that not only will the American consumer suffer, but I am convinced that the free enterprise system will suffer, and that is really disturbing to me.

BORK

It may be that you are right, Senator, and maybe the evidence will show up. But let me say something about these companies whose prices all go up at the same time. That happens in the wheat industry. You can have a thousand sellers and their prices will all go up at the same time. That is because they are responding to the same supply and demand conditions.

If I walked by on a street corner and people are standing there and everyone has an umbrella over his head, if it is not raining I think there is a conspiracy. If it is raining, I think they are all responding to the same conditions. And I think that is what we are talking about here.

Sure all the oil prices go up about the same time. So do the wheat prices. So do the hamburger prices.

METZENBAUM

They tell me my time is up. You and I will have further time to discuss this.

BORK

No. I do not want to discuss it anymore. I just want to say one thing. I never suggested that the law would allow just two companies to be left. I may have said I thought two companies would be enough for competition, but I do not think the mood of Congress in passing section 7 of the Clayton Act would allow me to do that.

CHAPTER FOUR

THE BILL OF RIGHTS

Although a major goal of conservatives was to overturn previous decisions that had used the Fourteenth Amendment to put states under First Amendment restrictions, that did not become a major issue in the Bork hearings. The nominee, in an exchange with Senator Heflin, made clear that he did not intend to tinker with the idea of incorporation.

Those not committed to his confirmation worried that he might achieve the same effect by significantly narrowing the First Amendment and by reading other portions of the Bill of Rights in a similarly restrictive fashion. That would free state and local communities to remove some of the freedoms many Americans thought they had. It would also allow the national government greater latitude in restricting liberty. Bork's view of the Ninth Amendment was indicative of this narrow reading.

Thus the meaning of liberty, either under the Constitution or as a natural right, became central to the debate over Bork's confirmation. He envisioned liberty as the right of the majority to decide standards and to chart the course society would take. Some Senators saw liberty as the constitutional protection of an individual's rights from abuses by that majority.

Bork's writings on free speech were subjected to critical review during this portion of the hearings. Earlier he had held a narrow view of free speech, applying it only to that speech involved in the political process, limited further by the type of action advocated by the speech. That position was seemingly modified during the course of the hearings, as were his views on other subjects, leading Sen. Leahy to refer to these changes as a "confirmation conversion."

The focal point of the free speech controversy was *Brandenburg v. Ohio* (1969), protecting the First Amendment rights of Klansmen and extending free speech to utterances bordering on imminent lawless action. Bork's condemnation of *Brandenburg* elicited concern from several Senators, who were also disturbed by his attacks on the hallowed Holmes/Brandeis position on free speech.

THE TESTIMONY

On Liberty

THURMOND

Judge Bork, you have written that, and I quote: "One of our constitutional freedoms or rights clearly given in the text is the power to govern ourselves democratically. Every time a court creates a new constitutional right against government or expands without warrant an old one, the constitutional freedom of citizens to control their lives is diminished."

Could you elaborate on why this reasoning leads you to conclude that activist judges will not truly expand rights and freedoms, but instead will merely redistribute them?

BORK

The Constitution clearly gives majorities the right to rule large areas of life simply because they are majorities. That is a freedom, that is a liberty, of the majority. The Constitution also says there are some things no majority should be allowed to do to a minority or to an individual. That is fine. That is known as the resolution of what has been called "James Madison's dilemma."

But if a judge steps into an area that the Constitution says is for majorities and says the majority may not do these things, despite what the Constitution says, then he has taken away a majority freedom and placed it in the minority. That is merely a redistribution of liberty, not an increase of it.

SIMON

In a speech at Berkeley in 1985, you said: "What a court adds to one person's constitutional rights it subtracts from the rights of others." Do you believe that is always true?

BORK

Yes. I think it's a matter of plain arithmetic. I think our Constitution gives a constitutional right or a liberty, in areas where the Bill of Rights or the Civil War amendments can't prohibit it, to citizens to sit down and elect their representatives and make their laws.

If a court strikes down such laws on behalf of a plaintiff claiming a liberty, it automatically deprives the first group of its liberty. So what you're talking about here is a redistribution of liberty.

That seems to me to be arithmetically solid. I don't think there is any way you can get around it. But if the Constitution says the majority doesn't have that liberty, they shouldn't. Where it says they do have that liberty, they should.

SIMON

But that arithmetic equation isn't always quite true. If you give slaves freedom, using your analogy, you then take away the freedom of slave owners.

BORK

That is a redistribution of liberties, commanded by the Thirteenth Amendment to the Constitution. I certainly have no objection to a redistribution of liberties whenever the Constitution requires it or authorizes it. No objection whatsoever.

What I was talking about was judges who make up new liberties and say that they are expanding liberty. Well, they are for some people, but they're contracting it for other people.

SIMON

When you take away the liberty of a slave owner to have slaves, and grant liberty to those who are slaves, while I suppose you are taking one right away from the slave owner, the disparity is so great that it is important that that liberty be granted.

BORK

Oh, it is. I entirely agree with you.

SIMON

So when you say "I think it's a matter of plain arithmetic—"

BORK

Well, obviously, if you tell somebody he has a right against somebody else, the other person loses something. That's standard legal analysis. I don't think there's any question about it.

The fact is that in the case of slavery, we have the Thirteenth Amendment because we thought it was important to give slaves rights. We have the Fourteenth Amendment because we thought it was important to give former slaves rights, and the Fifteenth Amendment on voting rights was because we wanted to shift power or rights away from a ruling class that had it and give it to an underclass that needed it.

I have no objection to that. I just say that one must recognize that when a community passes a law because it wants to prohibit something, and the court says that law is invalid, it gives the people who object to the law liberty and takes it away from the folks who wanted the law.

That's fine, and I like it, if it's in the Constitution. The Constitution itself redistributes rights and it's intended to, and it should. The only thing I have ever objected to was the court doing it without constitutional authority.

SIMON

But when you look at the Constitution, you're not looking at the Tax Code. If you're writing a Tax Code, and if you grant some group 1 billion dollars worth of exemptions, you eliminate 1 billion over on the other side. You recognize that?

BORK

Of course. But I was not saying that the liberties of the two groups are of equal value. We redistribute liberties all of the time, not only through the Constitution but through statutes, regulations and so forth. That's the way government operates.

But what I was objecting to in that speech was the rhetoric, that every time the Court makes up a new right, it enlarges liberty. It does for one group, but it diminishes it for another group.

SIMON

My concern is you seem to almost equate the two.

BORK

If the Constitution says you may not do this to this minority, and the Constitution says that frequently about various kinds of minorities, then that's fine. The Constitution has made the determination the rights are to be there and not with the larger group. That's exactly what constitutional law is about.

If a court, without guidance from the Constitution, says to an individual or a minority that "you may not be regulated in this way," then the court has redistributed the liberties without authority from the Constitution. It is wrong to say they have just increased liberty. They may or they may not. They've certainly redistributed liberty.

A court has no authority to do that without constitutional mandate.

SIMON

I have long thought that it is fundamental in our society that when you expand the liberty of any of us, you expand the liberty of all of us.

BORK

I think, Senator, that is not correct.

For example, if a community decides that it wants to ban certain forms of obscenity, because that obscenity impacts on their children, their family life and attitudes and the moral environment, and if a court should come along and say you may not ban that obscenity, so that the practice of showing obscene materials increases, I think the majority has lost some liberties. Not everybody's liberty has been expanded.

We can differ about that, but it seems to me fairly evident. One of the great liberties we have is to govern ourselves through representative bodies like the Senate and the House of Representatives. If a court takes that away from us, we've lost a liberty. A court ought to take it away from us if the Constitution says so. It ought not if the Constitution does not say so. It should leave us the liberty of electing our Representatives and Senators and having them make public policy for us.

SIMON

Then we are back to the exchange you had with Senator Specter here, where you go back to original intent. You accept precedent for the Chinese, for others, under the equal protection clause. But you are not willing to create the precedent in behalf of liberty.

BORK

Yes, I am, under the equal protection clause. Once you begin to operate, as the Court has, and as John Paul Stevens suggests, with a reasonable basis test which would produce the same results in race and gender, as the Court currently gets through its multi-tier analysis, then as various challenges come up under the equal protection clause, the question will be whether this is a reasonable distinction or whether it's an outmoded stereotype of some sort.

If a new challenge is made by a new group, then I would create precedent, obviously, if I apply that test as I said I would. The Constitution says any person is protected under the equal protection clause. If you look at the language, which an original intention person should, I think you're driven to a reasonable basis test.

I am sure that the framers of that Fourteenth Amendment did not think that the way women were treated in those days was unreasonable. That was to them very natural. As women's place in society has changed, all of those distinctions that they made and thought were entirely reasonable now look to us unreasonable. That's the way constitutional doctrine evolves.

SIMON

I recognize you have changed your opinions from this Indiana Law Review article, which you have heard more about in the last three days than you probably want to, but let me just read a few sentences here.

"Compare the facts in *Griswold* with a hypothetical suit by an electric utility company and one of its customers to void a smoke pollution ordinance as unconstitutional. The cases are identical." "It is clear that the court cannot make the necessary distinction."

Do you really believe that in one case, where a couple uses contraceptives and the majority in the court rules that that is unconstitutional, that that is really identical with an electric utility company violating a smoke pollution ordinance?

BORK

If I were a legislator, I would clearly vote for the smoke pollution ordinance and I would vote against the anti-contraceptive ordinance, and as a citizen I would oppose the anti-contraceptive statute and I would vote for the smoke pollution statute.

I am talking here about two cases in which, if there is no constitutional objection to either statute, then a judge has no way of imposing his moral preferences upon the Constitution. The judge may not have a hierarchy of values that does not come from the Constitution. He may not say to a consumer: "You value your low-cost electricity, but that's an ignoble value, whereas the other is a noble value" unless the Constitution tells him to make that choice.

A legislator can make that moral distinction because a legislator is responsive to the people and must make moral choices all the time. A judge is supposed to enforce the morality of the people who made the law, in this case, the Constitution. That is the only reason I say the judge has no way to tell those two cases apart if the Constitution does not speak.

SIMON

But that gets back to whether you use the Constitution to expand liberty. My hope is that the courts, through the decades ahead, will, where it is prudent, see that we can expand liberty, the right of privacy and other things.

My concern, as I look at your record and a host of things, is you are moving, perhaps somewhat reluctantly, and if not reluctantly, then after the fact, accepting the decisions and the precedents of the Court, but not leading in seeing that people have these rights.

Is that an inaccurate reading of the record?

BORK

The difficulty with the record is that I wrote only about what I regarded as excesses by the Supreme Court. I did not write about the ones that I approved. As a matter of fact, over the years I don't suppose I was criticizing more than one or two Supreme Court cases a year. When they made a proper expansion of liberty, I did not sit down and write an approving article. Perhaps I should have. It was only when I thought a principle or a mode of decision that was coming into the law was not justified that I wrote an article.

That is why you will not see the other side. But, you know, I approve of most Supreme Court opinions. Some of them expand liberty.

SIMON

My concern is that I do not want someone on the Court who is going to be so rigid in the application of liberty that there is not some expansion and growth in liberty for the people of this country.

BORK

I have a good record on civil rights and constitutional rights. I do not believe that constitutional freedom should be given a narrow or a crabbed construction, and I have never given such a narrow or a crabbed construction to them. In fact, just the other day, a case came down in which I reversed a new sentence on double jeopardy grounds. That, I should say, before somebody makes the accusation that has been made, was a case that was voted on and assigned to me long before this nomination came up.

You look at my opinions, and you will see no reason to expect any crabbed or narrow interpretation of any clause. Those clauses have to evolve as circumstances, technologies and other things change, so that they are given their full and fair value.

SPECTER

Does not the view that you express with some repetitiveness in your speeches about an uneasiness or an opposition to egalitarian principles, which you equate with permissiveness, really have a very significant effect upon your own judicial philosophy?

BORK

I do not think so. For one thing, when I am talking about these matters I am usually complaining about going too far toward equality of result. I never have any problem with equality of opportunity. I understand that even more equality of result than free process would give us is desirable. Some redistribution is desirable, and it is not for me as a judge to judge the degree of redistribution.

As far as the equal protection clause is concerned, I do not regard that as requiring equality of result. I regard that as requiring equality of opportunity, if that distinction makes any sense in that context.

The Fourteenth Amendment and Incorporation of the Bill of Rights

HEFLIN

I do not recall that anyone has questioned you about the concept of incorporating certain parts of the Bill of Rights into the due process clause of the Fourteenth Amendment.

That has been a highly debated and controversial area of jurisprudence, particularly with the Warren Court, and there were efforts made, first, to go through the privileges and immunities clause. Then they developed the concept of the due process clause.

Would you give us your feelings of whether or not this was judicial activism, judicial imperialism, or what is your feeling pertaining to the reasoning that took place in the selective incorporation theory?

BORK

The historical evidence on that is still coming in. When I first went into teaching, the received wisdom was the article by Professor Fairman, in the Stanford Law Review, arguing that there really was not any historical evidence for incorporation. He was responding to Justice Black's opinion in the area. Since then there has been more evidence that incorporation was intended.

When we say "incorporation," we are talking about the theory that the due process clause of the Fourteenth Amendment applies against the States the Bill of Rights, which originally applied only to the federal government. Since then there has been more evidence that incorporation was intended. It is very clear that Congressman Bingham, who wrote much of the clause and managed it in the House, and Senator Howard, who was a member of the committee that drafted it and was the floor manager in the Senate, clearly intended to incorporate not just the Bill of Rights but any personal protection to be found in the Constitution.

So there is some pretty good historical evidence that it was intended. There is an argument whether the ratifying conventions understood that or not. I do not know the answer to that, but it seems to me that now the Court has done it that there is some evidence that what they did was correct.

In any event, it seems to me a beneficial development and thoroughly established, and I do not think anybody really wants to see the States free of the Bill of Rights. There is considerable historical evidence that it was intended, some that it was not.

I have never written about it. I have never examined the original sources. I think there is some historical support for it. It is a thoroughly established doctrine and it will stay that way.

As you know, Justice Black, who objected strongly to what he called the natural law/due process version of making law, in fact incorporated various parts of the Bill of Rights, now almost all of the Bill of Rights, against the States through the Fourteenth Amendment. In large part his motive for doing that was to prevent judges from roaming at will. He thought if you could incorporate the Bill of Rights against the States, then judges would apply the prohibition to the Bill of Rights and secure liberty, but they would not use what he called the natural law method of making up rights.

On that point, Senator, reasonable men can differ. Strong arguments can be made on both sides. I adhere to my view that I want judges to be confined by the law, not make it up. There are others who disagree with that, but I believe in interpreting it, not creating it.

SPECTER

It is true that the specific provisions of the Bill of Rights were taken into the due process clause of the Fourteenth Amendment. But that was not the sole basis used by the Court. Before the Court came to the incorporation doctrine, there were many wrangles. And the first time the Supreme Court interfered, or took jurisdiction of and changed, a State criminal proceeding was the very famous case of *Brown v. Mississippi*. If you read through that case, a 1936 opinion of the Supreme Court, it is an abject horror story. I am not going to go through the facts. Sufficient to quote Chief Justice Hughes' characterization of it as a medieval account as to what was done to the black defendant in that case by the law enforcement authorities of Mississippi.

The Court then, for the first time, strikes down a State criminal conviction on the ground that it offends principles of justice rooted in the tradition and conscience of our people, so as to be ranked as fundamental. And that got it started.

Free Speech and The First Amendment

LEAHY

As I understand the *Finzer* case, that involved a statute, passed by Congress, which says basically that if you are going to have somebody demonstrating within 500 feet of an embassy, they can do that only if their demonstration is favorable to the policies of that government. Is that, in laymen's language, basically what it says?

BORK

That's right. The first part of the statute says it's unlawful to display any placard designed to bring into public odium any foreign government or to bring into public disrepute political, social, economic acts of any foreign government. That's right.

LEAHY

You could, however, display a placard which was supportive of that government.

BORK

That's correct.

LEAHY

It's interesting, because really what you do with such a statute is an unusual twist. Let's take a hypothetical. We have the embassy of Iraq, and after the Iraq air force had nearly destroyed the USS *Stark*, killing more than 30 Americans, according to that statute you could have somebody down there with a placard saying to the Iraqi Government we agree with everything you did, right on. But if the mother and father of one of those sailors killed wanted to stand down there with a placard and say we think this was a heinous, murderous act, they couldn't do it.

BORK

Under the statute, that is correct.

LEAHY

I realize this matter is up before the Supreme Court, and they will have to decide it. In some ways I would find that virtually unconstitutional on its face in allowing one type of speech but not the other. It would be one thing to say for security you don't allow people to congregate within a certain distance of an embassy. I can understand that.

BORK

I dealt with that point in the opinion. I guess I better not argue it further. But, of course, Congress is free now or any other time to say no expression of opinion about a foreign government may be had within 200 feet, 300 feet, whatever.

LEAHY

Wouldn't that be more acceptable than to say you can have one kind but not the other, and tell Americans that they can say one sort of thing about a foreign government but not something else?

BORK

Americans can say anything they want to about Iraq, anything hostile they want to say about Iraq or any other foreign government, or the U.S. Government; just not within 500 feet of the embassy of that government.

LEAHY

The point I make concerns me very much. A court upholding a statute which says to Americans you can say certain things but not other things. It's one thing to say you can't say anything within a certain distance but to say you can say some things but not other things — that I find of great concern.

BORK

It is a matter of concern. I agree with you about that, and I tried to deal with that concern. In a way, saying you may not say anything is a more restricting statute than saying you may not insult a foreign government.

LEAHY

I find it more chilling to say that we will select what can be said.

Let me show you a couple of books. I am not really trying to plug anybody here, but the one on the right is Speaker O'Neill's latest book. It is on the best seller list.

The Post says: "The former Speaker of the House recounts half a century in public life as a bread-and-butter liberal." The other is on the nonfiction paperback best seller list, "Fatherhood" by Bill Cosby. It is described in the reviews as an actor on the subject of children.

Let's assume neither book is obscene.

BORK

I am willing to assume that.

LEAHY

I have not read either one of them, but I will assume that, too. Does it make any difference in First Amendment protection that this one is obviously political and this one of Mr. Cosby's is not?

BORK

Under settled law it does not and I accept it. It seems to me that the settled law is now that the person writing the book does not have to prove that it is political or any way connected to politics. The government has to prove it is obscene.

LEAHY

So if we were dealing with, at least by the title of it, something, a movie, on the one hand, "The Making of the Constitution," and the other one, "Revenge of the Nerds," at least by the title it does not make any difference?

BORK

No. That does not make any difference, and I have seen so many movies about the Constitution that I would now choose the second movie.

SPECTER

Let me move ahead to the underpinnings of the clear and present danger test, and let me read a very short extract from Holmes' dissenting opinion in *Abrams*. This is really the essence of the First Amendment freedom of speech, and this is the doctrine which you have characterized as being "internally inconsistent" and being "terrifying frivolity."

"Men may come to believe that the ultimate good desired is better reached by free trade in ideas, that the best test of truth is the power of the thought to get itself accepted in the competition of the market, and that truth is the only ground upon which their wishes safely can be carried out. That, at any rate, is the theory of our Constitution."

Now you very strongly criticized the Holmes statement in your Michigan Law Review speech, and you say this:

"There is doubt about even the proviso, for Holmes could bring himself to write in *Gitlow*, and Brandeis to join him, that, 'If in the long run the beliefs expressed in proletarian dictatorship are destined to be accepted by the dominant forces of the community, the only meaning of free speech is that they should be given their chance and have their way.' That statement defies explanation."

It seems to me, Judge Bork, in studying the long line of cases on freedom of speech, that the essence of a lusty debate and full discourse is to let it go on and on until you reach the point of imminent violence. If there is imminent violence, then there is a clear and present danger, and it becomes wrongful conduct, and it becomes criminal conduct.

But even where the proponent argues the proletarian dictatorship, as much as we dislike it, we say, go ahead. Even if the proponent says, "Let's have a revolution to get there," which is the advocacy of lawlessness which you also condemn, that seems to me to be within the Holmes doctrine and a proper description of the law and the spirit of freedom of speech. If the person has to resort to violence in a democratic society, it shows the absurdity of his position, when he doesn't need under our system to resort to violence.

But as long as it is mere words, he ought to be permitted to say it, as I read the cases and get the feel of the First Amendment. Freedom of speech is really the core value, and is hardly frivolous.

BORK

Senator, Holmes' reasoning defies explanation on his own terms. He is saying, and in this first part I agree with him entirely, that the First Amendment is intended to protect free trade in ideas, and the test of their truth is their acceptance in the marketplace of ideas. That is fine.

Then he says it is all right for people to advocate revolution, to advocate violence by which a minority will seize the government and shut off the marketplace of ideas. He concludes that by saying:

"If, in the long run, the beliefs expressed in proletarian dictatorship are destined to be accepted by the dominant forces of the community, the only meaning of free speech is they should be given their chance and have their way."

"Dominant forces in the community" is not a majority voting for proletarian dictatorship, and the man who was speaking there was not advocating an election to put in proletarian dictatorship. He was advocating violence to close the marketplace of ideas, to stop the free trade in ideas.

It seems to me you can't get from "the most wonderful thing about our society is the free trade in ideas" to "it's all right for this fellow to try to get people to overthrow the government so that they can close the free trade in ideas."

SPECTER

I disagree categorically, if you don't get to the point where violence is imminent. A proletarian dictatorship is a terrible system as you and I see it, but on the merits, let him argue it.

BORK

Oh, I would let him argue it.

SPECTER

You would let him argue the proletarian dictatorship?

BORK

Oh, sure, I would let him argue it.

SPECTER

Why not let him argue violence if it doesn't come to a point of inciting to violence? Isn't the very argument, itself, undercutting any rationality of the argument? As long as there is no violence that is imminent?

BORK

If you get a lot of these arguments going on you don't know when violence is imminent. A lot of this is conspiratorial and advocacy taking place in organizations that organize like military units.

It would be a defensible First Amendment position to say that whether or not there is a real danger to our form of government and to our freedoms and to our free speech posed by this kind of thing, advocacy of violence to close the marketplace of ideas is a legislative judgment, and they may choose to let that speech go forward or not. That was what I said then, and it seems to me it is a tenable philosophical position now.

However, I have also said that the settled law has become otherwise. The Holmes-Brandeis position has triumphed in the law.

I now accept, as a judge, the position that the law has reached, and I have no desire to overturn it. I have no desire to whittle it away. But that does not mean that I have abandoned my original critique of those theories. I haven't even thought about them again, much less abandoned them.

Our discussion of *Brandenburg* and clear and present danger demonstrates that I have not shifted from my writings. I have said that, as a judge, I accept those cases as precedent and will apply them. It's settled law. I haven't said that these writings were wrong. I have said that I accept that body of precedent and will apply it. That's all I've said.

SPECTER

That's the reason that judicial philosophy is so important. If you have a judicial philosophy, there is some predictability as to where you'll be when the next set of facts comes up which are different than *Brandenburg*. No two cases are identical.

BORK

That's right.

SPECTER

The application of a legal philosophy very much depends upon the way it is held, and that's why, if you still disagree philosophically with *Brandenburg*, and you still disagree philosophically with the clear and present danger test, that raises a question in my mind as to how you will apply it to the next set of facts.

BORK

Well, I'll apply it as honestly as I can. That's all I can say to you.

The Ninth Amendment

DECONCINI

Do you have an opinion on the Ninth Amendment?

BORK

I think the Ninth Amendment may be a direct counterpart to the Tenth Amendment. The Tenth says, in effect, that power not delegated to the United States is reserved to the States or to the people.

I think the Ninth says that, like powers, the enumeration of rights shall not be construed to deny or disparage rights retained by the people in their State Constitutions. That is the best I can do with it.

DECONCINI

You feel that it only applies to their State constitutional rights?

BORK

If anybody shows me historical evidence about what they meant, I would be delighted. I just do not know.

DECONCINI

I do not have any historical evidence. What I want to ask you is purely hypothetical, Judge. Do you think it is unconstitutional for the Supreme Court to consider a right that is not enumerated in the Constitution?

BORK

There are two parts to that. First, there are some rights that are not enumerated but are found because of the structure of the Constitution and government. That is fine with me. That is a legitimate mode of constitutional analysis.

I do not think you can use the Ninth unless you know something of what it means. For example, if you had an amendment that says "Congress shall make no" and then there is an ink blot and you cannot read the rest of it and that is the only copy you have, I do not think the court can make up what might be under the ink blot if you cannot read it.

DECONCINI

If you had to speculate, what do you think Madison or some of the framers had in mind as to unenumerated rights?

BORK

They might have had in mind what I just said about the enumeration of these does not entitle judges to override the state constitutional rights. They also might have had in mind perhaps a fixed category of what they regarded as natural rights. I am a little surprised they did not spell it out and put it into the Constitution, because they specified all the other rights.

There is no evidence that I know of that this was to be a dynamic category of rights, that under the Ninth Amendment the court was free to make up more Bill of Rights. I think that had that been their objective, they could have spelled it out a lot better, and a lot of the constitutional debates we had, right after the Constitution was formed and John Marshall began applying the Constitution, would have been irrelevant because the court is just entitled to make up constitutional rights.

DECONCINI

Would you say that it would be unconstitutional for the Supreme Court to find a right — we will not say what it is, but Right A — because it is not enumerated here?

BORK

If the Supreme Court makes up a new right for which there is not historical evidence, then it has exceeded its powers under the Constitution.

THURMOND

You indicated that there are some rights that are not enumerated in the Constitution, but are recognized because of the structure of the Constitution and government. Could you give us an example of one of these?

BORK

The right to travel was first derived in *Crandall v. Nevada*, a couple of years before the Fourteenth Amendment was ratified.

Nevada was taxing people a dollar every time they left the State, and the Supreme Court struck down that tax in saying there was a right to travel without hindrance by the State, and it did so on structural reasoning about the nature of the Federal Union, and how you have to travel.

But the best example of structural reasoning in the law is Chief Justice Marshall's opinion in *McCulloch v. Maryland*, where, entirely on structural grounds, he first establishes the right of the United States to create a national bank, the Bank of the United States, and then establishes that that bank must be free from State taxation of its commercial instruments. An entirely structural, entirely sound argument.

The Death Penalty

SIMPSON

Let me ask you about the death penalty. Where do you find that in the Constitution?

BORK

As Solicitor General I made an oral argument and filed briefs as amicus for the United States in the case that brought the death penalty back after *Furman v. Georgia.* What you find in the Constitution is not only no prohibition of the death penalty, but you find repeated statements in the Constitution that the framers assumed the availability of the death penalty.

For example, the Fifth Amendment— "No person shall be held to answer for a capital crime, unless on presentment or indictment of a grand jury." A capital crime is the death penalty.

"Nor shall any person be subject for the same offense to be twice put in jeopardy of life or limb." If you are put in jeopardy of life, that is the death penalty.

"Nor shall any person be deprived of life, liberty or property without due process of law." Being deprived of life is the death penalty. The framers tell you that you have to have due process of law, but you can impose the death penalty.

The Fourteenth Amendment in 1868: "No State shall deprive any person of life, liberty, or property without due process of law." That is the death penalty again.

I think there is one more reference in the Constitution to the death penalty, Senator, but there are four, right there, that assume the availability of the death penalty so far as the Constitution is concerned.

CHAPTER FIVE

PRIVACY, ABORTION, AND STERILIZATION

The most critical issue that the public saw in the Court's immediate future was abortion. In a larger sense that involved the right of privacy. At the heart of the matter were two court decisions: *Griswold v. Connecticut* (1965) and *Roe v. Wade* (1973). In the former, Justice William O. Douglas had evolved a general right of privacy as a "penumbra" derived from the intent of several portions of the Bill of Rights.

Connecticut had adopted, long ago, a law banning the use or prescription of contraceptives. The law had apparently gone unenforced for years. Two officials of the Planned Parenthood League, one of them a licensed physician and a member of the Yale Medical School faculty, were fined for dispensing birth control information, instruction and advice to married couples. They appealed, and Douglas's opinion for the majority established a far-reaching right that was expanded in *Roe* to guarantee a right to abortion, though the *Roe* decision still left the states with some regulatory power.

In *Griswold*, dissenting Justices Hugo Black and Potter Stewart represented the position held by Bork. Bork's critics, fearing that he would reject the right of privacy and open the door to overturn *Roe*, were disturbed by his views on the constitutional right to privacy.

Related to privacy were two other cases which permitted a further exploration of Bork's view: *Skinner v. Oklahoma* (1942) and *Oil, Chemical & Atomic Workers International Union v. American Cyanamid Co.* (1984). Both cases are discussed at length in the testimony that follows.

In *American Cyanamid* Bork wrote the unanimous opinion for the court of appeals. The facts in the case were badly garbled in the hearings: OSHA had fined Cyanamid for imposing a "hazard" — its sterilization proposal. The OSHA Review Board had overruled OSHA, and the Administrative Judge had agreed with the review board, a position upheld by Bork's court upon appeal. The campaign to deny Bork a seat on the Supreme Court played heavily on Bork's alleged insensitivity to women as exemplified by this case.

THE TESTIMONY

Privacy

BIDEN

Let's talk about the *Griswold* case. While you were living in Connecticut, that State had a law that made it a crime for anyone, even a married couple, to use birth control. You indicated that you thought that law was "nutty," to use your words, and I quite agree. Nevertheless, Connecticut, under that "nutty" law, prosecuted and convicted a doctor and the case finally reached the Supreme Court.

The Court said that the law violated a married couple's constitutional right to privacy. You criticized this opinion in numerous articles and speeches, beginning in 1971 and as recently as July 26th of this year. In your 1971 article, "Neutral Principles and Some First Amendment Problems," you said that the right of married couples to have sexual relations without fear of unwanted children is no more worthy of constitutional protection by the courts than the right of public utilities to be free of pollution control laws.

You argued that the utility company's right or gratification to make money and the married couple's right or gratification to have sexual relations without fear of unwanted children are identical. It appears to me that you are saying that the government has as much right to control a married couple's decision about choosing to have a child or not, as that government has a right to control the public utility's right to pollute the air. Am I misstating your rationale here?

BORK

With due respect, Mr. Chairman, I think you are. I was making the point that where there is no provision in the Constitution that applies to the case then a judge may not say: "I place a higher value upon a marital relationship than I do upon an economic freedom." Only if the Constitution gives him some reasoning. Once the judge begins to say economic rights are more important than marital rights or vice versa, and if there is nothing in the Constitution, the judge is enforcing his own moral values, which I have objected to.

I was objecting to the way Justice Douglas, in *Griswold*, derived this right. It may be possible to derive an objection to an anti-contraceptive statute in some other way. I do not know.

But starting from the assumption that there is nothing in the Constitution, in any legitimate method of constitutional reasoning about either subject, all I am saying is that the judge has no way to prefer one to the other and the matter should be left to the legislatures who will then decide which competing gratification, or freedom, should be placed higher.

All that means is that the judge may not choose.

BIDEN

Who does?

BORK

The legislature.

BIDEN

Does a State legislative body have a right to pass a law telling a married couple that behind their bedroom door they can or cannot use birth control?

BORK

There is always a rationality standard in the law, Senator. I do not know what rationale the State would offer or what challenge the married couple would make. I have never decided that case. If it ever comes before me, I will have to decide it. All I have done was point out that the right of privacy, as defined or undefined by Justice Douglas, was a free-floating right that was not derived in a principled fashion from constitutional materials.

What I objected to was the way in which this right of privacy was created and that was simply this. Justice Douglas observed, quite correctly, that a number of provisions of the Bill of Rights protect aspects of privacy and indeed they do and indeed they should.

But he went on from there to say that since a number of the provisions did that and since they had emanations, by which I think he meant buffer zones to protect the basic right, he would find a penumbra which created a new right of privacy that existed where no provision of the Constitution applied.

BIDEN

You do not believe that there is a general right of privacy that is in the Constitution?

BORK

Not one derived in that fashion. There may be other arguments and I do not want to pass upon those.

BIDEN

Have you ever thought of any? Have you ever written about any?

BORK

Yes, as a matter of fact, Senator. I taught a seminar with Professor Bickel starting in about 1963 or 1964 called Constitutional Theory. I was then all in favor of *Griswold*. I thought that was a great way to reason. I tried to build a course around that, only I said we can call it a general right of freedom, and let's then take the various provisions of the Constitution, treat them the way a lawyer treats common law cases, extract a more general principle and apply that.

I did that for about 6 or 7 years, and Bickel fought me every step of the way. He said it was not possible. At the end of 6 or 7 years, I decided he was right.

BIDEN

It seems to me that if you cannot find a rationale for the decision of the *Griswold* case, then all the succeeding cases are up for grabs.

BORK

I have never tried to find a rationale and I have not been offered one. Maybe somebody would offer me one. I do not know if the other cases are up for grabs or not.

I have written that some of these cases were wrongly decided. For some of them I can think of rationales that would make them correctly decided but wrongly reasoned. One of the problems with the right of privacy, as Justice Douglas defined it, or did not define it, is not simply that it comes out of nowhere, that it does not have any rooting in the Constitution. It is also that he does not give it any contours, so you do not know what it is going to mean from case to case.

KENNEDY

I believe, Mr. Bork, that in your world, the individuals have precious few rights to protect them against the majority and I think this is where the Bill of Rights comes in and what the Bill of Rights is all about, that there are some things in America which no majority can do to the minority or to the individuals. The provisions of the Fourteenth Amendment under section 1, include "nor shall any State deprive any person of life, liberty or property without the due process of law."

Isn't included in the concept of liberty, the right to privacy? In reading that term with the Ninth Amendment, which provides that "the enumeration in the Constitution of certain rights shall not be construed to deny or disparage others retained by the people," I would be interested in your reaction or response because it seems to me that the issues of privacy have been carefully enshrined within the Constitution by court decisions over the period of the last 60 years.

They are rights which are enshrined in such a way and respected and valued so importantly that I think Americans would have serious questions, I certainly do, about placing someone on the Supreme Court that is willing to find some kind of a rationale not to respect it.

BORK

I have the greatest respect for the Bill of Rights and I will enforce the Bill of Rights. I have enforced the Bill of Rights. What we were talking about here was a generalized, undefined right of privacy which is not in the Bill of Rights. As I said in my opening statement, a judge has to apply the law and the law comes from the text, the history and the structure of the Constitution.

There are important aspects of privacy in the Bill of Rights. This Congress has increased privacy in many ways by statute. As a society, we value it, but as a judge I do not think I can tell the American people they may not have a law that in no way conflicts with the written and historical Constitution.

Let me repeat about this created, generalized and undefined right of privacy in *Griswold*. Aside from the fact that the right was not derived by Justice Douglas in any traditional mode of constitutional analysis, we do not know what it is. We do not know what it covers. It can strike at random. For example, the Court has not applied the right of privacy consistently and I think it is safe to predict that the Court will not.

If it really is a right of sexual freedom in private, as some people have

suggested, then *Bowers v. Hardwick*, which upheld a statute against sod-
omy as applied to homosexuals, is wrongly decided. Privacy to do what,
Senator? Privacy to use cocaine in private? Privacy for businessmen to
fix prices in a hotel room? We just do not know what it is.

Privacy was not the issue in that case. It was the use of contraceptives, and it is a little hard to locate something about contraceptives in
the Constitution.

But be that as it may, let me illustrate my objection to what is generalized "right of privacy." Suppose a Senator introduced a bill which said
every man, woman and child in this country has a right of privacy, period.
I do not think that bill would go anywhere until he had to tell everybody
exactly what the right of privacy protected. Did it protect incest? Did it
protect beating your wife in private? Did it protect price-fixing in private?

No Congress would ever pass a generalized right of privacy; make of
it what you will. No court would uphold such a statute because it would
be void for vagueness.

The Supreme Court or Justice Douglas in effect did the same thing
with the Constitution. Nobody knows what that thing means. But you
have to define it. And the court has not given it definition. That is my
only point.

The only reason that Connecticut statute stayed on the book — it
was an old, old statute — was that it was not enforced. If anybody had
tried to enforce that against a married couple, he would have been out
of office instantly and the law would have been repealed.

Furthermore, if the prosecutor brought such a case, I do not think
any court would uphold a conviction, assuming that you could get a conviction. That law had not been enforced for so long I think you would
have a great argument of no fair warning. It is so out of date it has gone
into limbo.

I think the law was an utterly silly law, but my objection is simply
to the undefined nature of what the Court did there. I have tried to il-

lustrate that for you by asking you whether you would vote for a statute that said nothing more than that everybody has a right of privacy, and the court shall enforce it. I do not think you would.

If I were a legislator, I would vote against that statute instantly.

DECONCINI

Right.

BORK

As a judge, I would have to be persuaded that there was something in the Constitution.

DECONCINI

Do you see anything else in the Constitution?

BORK

I have not gone through this exercise, Senator, so I am just speculating. The most likely form of attack might be the equal protection attack. I do not know.

BIDEN

Putting aside all the specific amendments you have mentioned during the past several days, do you believe that the Constitution recognizes a marital right to privacy?

BORK

I do not know. It may well. I have seen arguments to that effect, but I have never investigated that. It is certainly one that I entirely agree with. I mean, I agree with the concept, and I think it is very important that it be maintained.

But I have never worked on a constitutional argument in that area.

BIDEN

As you know, in *Griswold*, both the concurrent opinion and the lead opinion uses and refers to a marital right of privacy. It seems to me that you can't find that marital right in the First, the Fourth, the Fifth, the Eighth Amendments. The only place you can find it, that anybody has been able to find it, is either in the Ninth and/or in the Fourteenth Amendment, both of which either through substantive due process or through the Ninth Amendment, you reject —"reject" may be the wrong word — you are very leery of the use of the Ninth Amendment at all as you have outlined for us, and you don't like substantive due process.

So quite frankly, Judge, I don't see how you can find, by your theory, a marital right to privacy.

BORK

All right. As to the marital right of privacy, it is essential to a civilized society. I do not know of any state, including Connecticut, that has ever tried to interfere with it because even the law in Connecticut was never used — nobody ever went in and arrested a married couple for using contraceptives or even threatened it, and I do not think it could be enforced given the Fourth Amendment and given the lack of enforcement.

So I don't know. Offhand, I cannot construct, just sitting here, a constitutional argument. Maybe I could if I spent a few days at it, but I don't think it is a live issue because no state has ever tried to enforce such a law.

BIDEN

With the views you have now, had you been sitting on the Court, how would you have ruled on that case?

BORK

It is quite clear. I think marital privacy is a right older than the Bill of Rights, and that is why it has always been respected. Even in Connecticut, they didn't enforce that law against married couples and they had a terrible time, the Yale professors did, getting these doctors arrested.

It is a right deeply built into our society, no doubt about it. But, if I were sitting on the Court and Justice Douglas circulated that essay about emanations and penumbras resulting in a generalized right of privacy, which is wholly undefined and we don't know where it will go next — no, I would not have agreed to that opinion.

Merely the fact that it is a dumb law gives the Court no additional power because there is no statement in the Constitution that no State shall make a dumb law. You referred to the fact that when people are dissatisfied with legislatures and executives, they always look to the courts. It is also true that there is a great deal of dissatisfaction with the courts in this country.

Marital privacy is a very important thing. If a case came up in which I had to think about a constitutional principle, I would think very hard because it is so important. However, if when I was finished thinking I could make no legitimate constitutional case, I would not make a decision that was not justified by the Constitution.

BIDEN

My last question, a reiteration. You have indicated you wouldn't have voted with the majority in *Griswold*. Would you have voted with the minority?

BORK

If I had not seen a better argument than the one that Justice Douglas offered, I would have joined Justice Hugo Black and Justice Potter Stewart.

BIDEN

Have you ever seen a better argument?

BORK

I have never looked at an argument from that area again.

Roe v. Wade

HATCH

You have been criticized for having been critical of this abortion case, *Roe v. Wade*.

BORK

If *Griswold* established or adopted a privacy right on reasoning which was utterly inadequate, and failed to define that right so we know what it applies to, *Roe* contains almost no legal reasoning. We are not told why it is a private act and, if it is, why this one is protected. There are lots of private acts that are not protected. We get a review of the history of abortion and we get a review of the opinions of various groups like the American Medical Association, and then we get rules.

That's what I object to about the case. It does not have legal reasoning in it that roots the right to an abortion in constitutional materials.

HATCH

I presume your concerns about the reasoning of *Roe* do not necessarily mean that you would automatically reverse that case as a Justice of the Supreme Court?

BORK

No. If that case, or something like it, came up, and if the case called for a broad up or down, which it may not, I would first ask the lawyer who wants to support the right: "Can you derive a right of privacy, not to be found in one of the specific amendments, in some principled fashion from the Constitution so I know not only where you got it but what it covers?"

There are rights that are not specifically mentioned in the Constitution, like the right to travel. It's conceivable he could do that, I don't know. If he could not do that, I would say: "Well, if you can't derive a general right of privacy, can you derive a right to an abortion, or at least to a limitation upon anti-abortion statutes, legitimately from the Constitution?"

If after argument, that didn't sound like it was going to be a viable theory, I would say to him: "I would like you to argue whether this is the kind of case that should not be overruled." Because, obviously, there are cases we look back on and say they were erroneous or they were not compatible with original intent, but we don't overrule them for a variety of reasons.

As I said before, a judge with an original intent philosophy, which goes back, by the way, to Marshall and Joseph Story, needs a strong theory of precedent to keep from getting back into matters that are long settled, even if incorrectly settled.

HEFLIN

Let me quote some of your writings: *Roe v. Wade* is in itself an unconstitutional decision, a serious and wholly unjustifiable usurpation of legislative authority. Is that a correct recital of a statement you have made.

BORK

I made that statement, yes.

HEFLIN

What do you, at this time, see as a possibility of a limitation?

BORK

It would seem to me that it would be easier to argue a right to an abortion than it would be to find this generalized right of privacy. For example, I understand some groups are trying an equal protection argument.

Only women have this specific burden and forcing a woman to carry a baby to term, some of the groups are arguing, is a form of gender discrimination. I have not seen that argument worked out, but I know it is being worked on.

I do not suggest it would succeed. I do not suggest it would not. You asked me if one could begin to talk about where one might root such an argument, and I think you might attempt to root it there, successfully or not, I do not pretend to guess, but it is easier than a general right of privacy.

I do not mean to try to offer anybody some hope that I would find that constitutional right. I am just saying that that is one area in which the argument might take place. I do not think it is entirely contrary to my constitutional philosophy because I have been saying that the equal protection clause applies to women as well as to men and that, for over 90 years, the Supreme Court has been using this question of this is a reasonable, fair classification.

Sterilization

BIDEN

Let's talk about another basic right, the right not to be sterilized by the government. The Supreme Court addressed that right in *Skinner v. Oklahoma*. Under Oklahoma law, someone convicted of certain crimes faced mandatory sterilization. In 1942, Mr. Skinner, convicted of his third offense and facing sterilization, brought his case to the Supreme Court.

The Court said that the State of Oklahoma could not sterilize him: "We are dealing with legislation which involves one of the
basic civil rights of man. Marriage and procreation are fundamental
to the very existence and survival of a race. There is no redemption
for the individual whom the law touches. Any experiment which the
State conducts is to his irreparable injury. He is forever deprived of a
basic liberty."

Judge, you said that Supreme Court decision is improper and intellectually empty. Do you think that there is a basic right, under the
Constitution, not to be forcibly sterilized by the State?

BORK

There may well be, but not on the grounds stated there. I hate to keep
saying this, Mr. Chairman. Much of my objection is to the way some
members of the Court, not always the whole Court, have gone about
deriving these things. In *Skinner* it might have been better to say that
the statute does not have a reasonable basis because there is no scientific evidence upon which to rest the thought that criminality is really
genetically carried.

The second thing about that case is that Justice Douglas did say
something which is quite correct and he did not need to talk about
procreation and fundamental rights to do it. He noted that the statute
made distinctions between a robber and an embezzler. The embezzler
was not subject to this kind of thing.

Had he gone on and pointed out that those distinctions really sterilized, in effect, blue collar criminals and exempted white collar criminals,
and indeed, appeared to have some taint of a racial basis to it, he could
have arrived at the same decision in what I would take to be a more
legitimate fashion.

I think the sterilization statute would have failed under a reasonable
basis test.

BIDEN

So you have to find a reasonable basis. If there is one, you could sterilize. If there is not one, you cannot. It seems to me that it comes down to a basic difference. You do not believe the Constitution recognizes what I consider to be a basic liberty not to be sterilized.

BORK

I agree that that is a basic liberty, and I agree that family life is a basic liberty. But the fact is we know that legislatures can, constitutionally, regulate some aspects of sexuality.

BIDEN

True.

BORK

We know that legislatures do and can constitutionally regulate some aspects of family life. There is no question that these things are subject to some regulation. We have divorce laws, child beating laws. The question always becomes, under the equal protection clause, has the legislature a reasonable basis for the kind of thing it does here.

The sterilization law would probably require an enormous or perhaps impossible degree of justification.

The Supreme Court has never said that sterilization under some circumstances is unconstitutional. I am not saying that that is a good thing they have never said it. I just want to point out that they have never said that. In fact, they have upheld sterilization programs. Justice Holmes did in a famous opinion.

A statute provided for sterilization of folks who were mentally retarded, I think after one or two generations. Holmes dismissed the equal protection argument as the usual last resort of the constitutional argument and wrote the infamous line — I like Holmes but this is not one of his better days — "Three generations of imbeciles are enough."

SIMPSON

Justice Holmes said that? I think we ought to get him back here.

BORK

I think considering the alternative, he might be glad to come back and do this.

METZENBAUM

Judge Bork, in this hearing we have already talked about your views on one sterilization case.

There is another one I want to discuss with you, the *American Cyanamid* case that you decided in 1984.

American Cyanamid operated a department which exposed women to lead, a substance which causes harm to a developing fetus. The company offered the women of the department a horrible choice.

The women could quit their jobs, or, they could keep their jobs and be sterilized.

The company called this a fetus protection policy. It was really a policy of be sterilized or be fired. You wrote the opinion allowing the company to maintain this policy.

There were 30 women working for the Cyanamid company when the company adopted the be-sterilized-or-fired policy. This policy forced 23 of those women to be sterilized or be fired. Five were actually sterilized before the lawsuit was filed. Cyanamid forced over 75 percent of their women employees to choose between their jobs and the possibility of ever having children.

Judge, I must tell you that it is such a shocking decision, and I cannot understand how you as a jurist could put women to the choice of work or be sterilized, and I would think you are entitled to comment on how you arrived at that decision.

BORK

I would be glad to. I am just trying to recall the case. That was a unanimous decision joined in by Judge Scalia — now Justice Scalia — and Senior District Judge Williams from California.

As I wrote, it is important to understand the context in which this case arose and the task that is set for this court. American Cyanamid found, and the administrative law judge agreed, that it could not reduce ambient lead levels in one of its departments sufficiently to eliminate the risk of serious harm to fetuses carried by women employees.

The company was thus confronted with unattractive alternatives. It could remove all women of child bearing age from that department — a decision that would have entailed discharging some of them and giving others reduced pay at other jobs — or the company could attempt to mitigate the severity of this outcome by offering continued employment in the department to women who were sterilized.

The company chose the latter alternative and the women involved were thus faced with a distressing choice. Some chose sterilization. Some did not. The fact is, if they had not offered that choice, these women would have been put in lower paying jobs or would have been discharged. They offered a choice to the women. Some of them, I guess, did not want to have children.

My opinion is not an endorsement of a sterilization policy. As I noted in the opinion, the policy might be an unfair labor practice or a form of employment discrimination under Title VII. Indeed, the union and the women employees had sued the employer under Title VII and had reached a settlement with that employer.

The basis of the decision was Congress' intent. Since the words of the act, "recognized hazards," were somewhat ambiguous, we looked at legislative history and cases interpreting similar language in other federal laws. My opinion concluded that Congress had been concerned with physical conditions of the workplace, not with policies offering women a choice.

My opinion was narrow. I said that the case might be different if the employer had offered the choice of sterilization in order to maintain an unlawfully high lead level, but the fact is the company could not get the lead levels down and the company was charged only because it offered women a choice.

That is not a pro sterilization opinion. It is not an anti-woman opinion. It is simply upholding a federal agency to which we owe deference in deciding. When you review a federal agency you are supposed to defer to their judgment if it is not outside the bounds of rationality — and the union conceded in oral argument that the company could lawfully have stated that only sterile women would be employed in the department.

So this case is simply about offering women who did not want to be discharged or sent to lower paying jobs a choice. That is all it was about.

METZENBAUM

As I understand your opinion, you are saying that the Occupational Safety and Health Administration came in with the position. You know, I am sure, that the Labor Secretary said that the policy should be barred. And you cannot tell me, Judge, that any member of Congress said or thought that a safer workplace could be achieved at the expense of forced sterilization.

Congress said no hazards in the workplace, but you wrote an opinion which said it was okay for a company to achieve safety at the expense of women by preventing its female employees from ever having children. I have to say to you that that is a distortion of the statute beyond recognition. I think it is unfair. I think it is inhumane, and maybe it somehow explains the concerns that women of this country have and have evidenced about your appointment.

BORK

There was not a forced sterilization policy at all. The company merely said if you wish to stay in a place that is dangerous to a fetus, if you do this we will let you stay there. The company did not achieve safety at the expense of women. They could not get the lead levels down. The administrative agency specifically found — OSHA specifically found — that the company had no way of getting the levels down.

METZENBAUM

I do not wish to belabor the point, but I have been informed, and I do not know if this is fact, that the lead level could have been reduced had the company been willing to expend the necessary funds. I am not certain that that is accurate.

BORK

I am not either, Senator, because that was not in the case. The administrative law judge, as I recall, had found that the lead level could not be reduced, and we do not review factual findings unless there is no substantial evidence for it.

BIDEN

So OSHA came along and said this was a hazard. The Commission that reviews OSHA said it is not a hazard. The Court agreed with the Commission that it was not a hazard.

BORK

Right. The Secretary of Labor could have appealed from the Commission decision but did not, and did not file a brief. If the position the

Commission took was so unacceptable, it is hard to see why the Secretary of Labor would not have appealed.

It was a sad choice these women employees had to make. It was very distressing. The only question was, should they be given a choice? And is giving them a choice a hazard? We did not think it was under the act.

HATCH

That had been reviewed by the Occupational Safety and Health Review Commission?

BORK

Yes.

HATCH

Who are experts in the field.

BORK

Yes, and we owed them some deference, too, in their interpretation of the law.

HATCH

But the important thing is how does the judge determine the technical, scientific questions like this except by relying on experts?

BORK

We did not rely upon the experts directly. We relied upon the finding of the administrative law judge who had heard the experts or had heard the evidence.

HATCH

Were you alone in this case or were you joined by another colleague?

BORK

I was joined by two other colleagues, one a visiting district judge from California and one Justice Scalia, then Judge Scalia.

HATCH

Scalia again. That guy seems to get you in trouble.

BORK

I am going to speak to him about this whole thing.

HATCH

You had better stay away from him. On second thought, maybe we had better get you there so you can have a good influence on him on the Court.

One further point. The company was charged with preventing any women of child-bearing age from being exposed to lead. Could the company have been charged with a legal violation if it had simply fired all the women in that department?

BORK

No, not under this statute. Everybody conceded that the company could have said women of child-bearing age are hereby fired. Or the company could have said women are transferred to another department. What the company did was give women a choice: You can be transferred to another department at a lower paying job or, if you want to, surgical sterilization is available to you. They just explained that there was that option.

If they had said any woman of child-bearing age is hereby discharged, there would have been no challenge. If the company had said that only sterile women will be employed, there would have been no argument about hazardous policy. It was merely the fact that the company said: "You have got to leave this place. If you do not want to, there is the option of sterilization." That is all that happened.

HATCH

It does seem to me that this sterilization policy might have been sex discrimination that is actionable under Title VII.

BORK

We said in the opinion it might be.

METZENBAUM

The women of America, in my opinion, have much to be worried about in connection with your appointment; the blacks as well. And it is only fair to say that you have made it quite clear in your appearance before this panel that you are not a frightening man, but you are a man with frightening views.

The basic problem is that to you the Constitution is not a living document; it is not a charter of liberty. And if you cannot find protection for the individual in the fine print, then the people of this country are out of luck.

You have stated views time again that would reverse progress for blacks, that would slam the door on women, that would allow government in the bedroom, that would adversely affect the rights of consumers, that would limit free speech, that would undercut the principle of equality under the law. And before we came to these hearings I had said publicly, and I repeat now, that I think you had the burden of proof on your shoulders to satisfy this committee that your views are consistent with the Bill of Rights and previous court decisions and the Constitution of the United States.

It is with some sadness, Judge Bork, that I say I really do not think you have done that.

Thank you very much.

BORK

Well, thank you, Senator. Let me respond briefly to that.

In the first place, it was a unanimous panel opinion and our court did not rehear this case en banc.

That means they did not think it was an outrageous case. It was a matter of statutory interpretation, not a matter of constitutional law, and I suppose the 5 women who chose to stay on that job with higher pay and chose sterilization were glad to have the choice that the company gave them.

I have never said anything or decided anything that should be frightening to women. You are undoubtedly correct, Senator, that there are women who are apprehensive. I think it can only be because they do not know my record. I have repeatedly showed you the cases I have decided on the court of appeals in which I have voted for women.

Now turn to the Constitution and my allegedly narrow views of that. If you will look at my First Amendment decisions you will see that I have taken a broad view of the First Amendment. If you will look at my decision that came down recently — and we voted that way long before I was nominated — I have taken a broad view of the double jeopardy clause in favor of a sentenced person.

If you will look at what I have stated about the equal protection clause, you will see it as a better view than one that a lot of people take who exclude groups from equal protection.

In sum, Senator, I think there is no basis for the concern you describe among women and blacks and I regret to say, I think there is no basis for the charges you have leveled at me.

METZENBAUM

Thank you, Judge Bork.

CHAPTER SIX

EQUAL PROTECTION

Bork's stand on equal protection was the best example of the dilemma his nomination created for many conservatives. Archconservatives sought a nominee who would undo much of the change that had taken place in civil rights since *Brown v. Board of Education* in 1954. While even the most hardened segregationist veterans (the best example was Strom Thurmond, who had been the symbol of segregation before *Brown*) no longer expected to have *Brown* reversed or the Fourteenth Amendment declared invalid, they were convinced that the role of the national government should be drastically reduced in areas involving women, minorities, criminal suspects, homosexuals and others.

Raoul Berger had led the intellectual attack on the liberal interpretation of the due process and equal protection clauses of the Fourteenth Amendment with publication of his *Government by Judiciary* in 1977. Conservatives longed for a nominee with Berger's attitudes. Specter, while not necessarily agreeing with Berger, had relied heavily on Berger in his questioning of Bork on original intent, and the Berger analysis of the meaning of the Fourteenth Amendment was evident in Specter's

continued effort to force Bork to reconcile the intent of the framers
with the decision in *Brown*.

Critics worried that Bork might exclude from Fourteenth Amendment protection all groups except blacks. To explore that concern, the
committee quizzed the nominee about the groups that Bork thought
were entitled to protection, and the degree of protection he would grant
them. His 1971 Indiana Law Review article was relevant here.

The examination of equal protection became the most confused and
incoherent section of the entire four and a half days that Bork was before the committee. Biden, at times, floundered in his attempt to understand the various levels of scrutiny that Bork said the Court had
applied to different groups — blacks, women, illegitimates, etc. — but
at least he tried to comprehend it. Most of the other Senators on the
panel remained silent. It is unlikely that their silence meant they so
fully understood the subject that questions were unnecessary. Another
explanation is more likely.

Even Bork seemed confused at times. Readers will note that despite Bork's effort to draw a line between "rational" and "reasonable," he
seemingly used the terms interchangeably. Biden's bewilderment is not
entirely the Senator's own fault.

Specter, however, diligently prodded Bork on this subject. The Spec-
ter-Bork exchange on the Fourteenth Amendment, as seen in chapter
one and here, is the best example of the law school debate that Simpson
said he so relished. Simpson, however, did not participate in this exchange.

In his account of this section of the hearings, Bork would write in
The Tempting of America that Specter simply could not comprehend
what Bork was saying about equal protection, the First Amendment
and a variety of other constitutional matters. A bitter Bork concluded
that "Because I was, out of necessity, patient with him, a lot of people
not versed in constitutional law got the impression that this was a seri-

ous constitutional discussion." Bork apparently did not share the view that this was a postgraduate seminar in constitutional law. From the testimony that follows readers can determine the depth of Specter's understanding and the level of the debate for themselves.

The phrase "discrete and insular minorities" came from *U.S. v. Carolene Products* (1938) and was the work of Justice Harlan Stone. The fullest development of the idea of various levels of scrutiny was put forth in *Craig v. Boren* (1955).

THE TESTIMONY

THURMOND

Let us start with the basics. The language says, "No State shall deny equal protection to any person." Does that mean every person in the State must be treated the same by every law?

BORK

It means every person in the State must be treated the same unless there is a valid basis for making a distinction. Obviously to take the extreme example, we do not treat burglars and honest people the same way. We make a strong distinction between those two groups, and that is a valid distinction.

When we come down to other groups, to other people, the question is whether the distinction made between them by a law is valid?

THURMOND

Naturally States draw distinctions among citizens. The Court must decide if the distinctions are reasonable under the Fourteenth Amendment. How does the Court do that?

BORK

The Supreme Court is a little bit divided on this issue. There are two schools of thought up there. One is that you identify a group and then decide what level of scrutiny you will give to any law that disadvantages that group in some way. That is a little paradoxical given the language of the amendment which means it applies to all persons so that no group could be excluded from the protection of the amendment.

What the equal protection clause requires is that people who are similarly situated be treated equally, and in the case of race, there is no valid basis for a distinction, and so the Fourteenth Amendment requires equality absolutely.

In the case of gender, there are only a few bases of distinction. For example, gender is irrelevant to your ability to work as a lawyer or as a doctor or anything else. I agree completely with the Supreme Court case of *Reed v. Reed*. A State statute said that if there is a man and a woman in the family, the one who is preferred, who becomes the administrator of an estate, must be the man. That is an irrational distinction and it was struck down, and it should have been.

The fact is, a reasonable basis approach [the second school of thought], which rejects artificial distinctions and discriminations, would arrive at virtually all of the same results that a majority of the Court has arrived at using a group approach and an intermediate level of scrutiny. There is really no difference in anything except the methodology, but women are covered, every person is covered, by the equal protection clause.

People seem to think that a reasonable basis test is a very weak protection. It is not. It has become a weak protection in economic areas because the Court has found distinctions there to be allowable that we do not allow elsewhere. But it is not a weak protection in areas of race, gender and so forth.

Let me point out what the Supreme Court has done in the past in this area. I disagree with the Court in these cases. In *Kotch v. Board of River Port Pilot Commissioners* — this is my Indiana article — the Court decided that a State could grant river boat pilots' licenses only to persons who were related by blood to existing pilots, and they could deny licenses to persons otherwise as well or better qualified. The Court upheld that ridiculous distinction not too long ago. That seems to me a distinction that would fail on a reasonable basis test.

Then in *Goesaert v. Cleary*, a case from 1948, the Court said that a State could refuse to license women as bartenders unless they are the wives or daughters of male owners of licensed liquor establishments.

That, too, is a ridiculous distinction and would fail under the reasonable basis test.

The reasonable basis test would give us all of the protections, maybe more, that you would get by identifying particular groups and deciding which level of scrutiny we get. I have just been shown Justice Stevens' remark in *City of Cleburne* which was a distinction about retarded children. It says, "In every equal protection case we have to ask certain basic questions. What class is harmed by the legislation, and has it been subjected to a tradition of disfavor by our laws? What is the public purpose that is being served by the law? What is the characteristic of the disadvantaged class that justifies the disparate treatment? In most cases, the answers to these questions will tell us whether the statute has a rational basis. The answers will result in the virtually automatic invalidation of racial classification and in the validation of most economic classifications, but they will provide differing results in cases involving classifications based on alienage, gender, or illegitimacy. But that is not because we apply an intermediate standard of review in those cases; rather, it is because the characteristics of these groups are sometimes relevant and sometimes irrelevant to a valid public purpose, or more specifically, to the purpose that the challenged law is purportedly intended to serve."

I think it is important to say that, because I think there has been a misimpression that the reasonable basis test is a weak test.

THURMOND

You have been accused of two errors in your analysis. First, you were charged with using a different standard for women. Is it not true that the current Court standard for gender cases is different than race cases?

BORK

The reasonable basis test is probably applied in both. It is just that the difference between races is irrelevant, and, therefore, distinctions may not be made.

That makes my point. There are very few areas in which a distinction between men and women is allowable. But that distinction would not be allowable on the basis of race.

THURMOND

You are accused of having a lower standard for gender and race cases than is currently employed.

BORK

That is not the case.

Let me say something about why I prefer a reasonable basis analysis to a group-by-group analysis. It is not just that the language of the amendment refers to "any person," therefore all persons. It is that if one thing is clear about the Fourteenth Amendment, it is that the framers of that amendment, the people who ratified it, had no intention of wiping out distinctions between men and women that we would now regard as very discriminatory. They went ahead and did it.

If you ask: "Group-by-group, are women included or not?" you have a hard time, as a matter of the intention of the people who passed that, saying women as a group are included. But we have been using a reasonable basis test as a means for implementing the broad language of the equal protection clause now for all of this century. I think it makes more sense.

Most of the distinctions that survive in the law are old ones made long ago which no longer seem reasonable to us. They are not reasonable. In a different state of culture, in a different state of society, they may have seemed reasonable. They are not now.

THURMOND

Judge Bork, comments have been made that you oppose certain rights of women. Justification for this attack is founded on your purported views that the equal protection clause should not be used to protect a woman's rights.

Do you feel that the equal protection clause is appropriate for the protection of women's rights, and would you please address this criticism?

BORK

At the time I wrote about the equal protection clause, the Court had never extended the clause to women. But in addition to that, the Court was in the process of saying it applies to blacks, it applies to illegitimate children, it applies to somebody else, and they were picking groups — which I thought was a wrong way to apply it. I think you apply it by requiring a reasonable basis for any distinction made between individuals or groups.

Now, in the case of race, it will be impossible, virtually, to find a reasonable distinction that will justify discrimination.

In the case of gender, it will depend on the particular issue. While it is possible to say in the area of race, no difference of treatment, it is not entirely possible to say that in the case of gender, simply because of physical differences. Combat — maybe the equal protection clause does not require that.

But in that sense, requiring a reasonable basis for any distinction made — yes, the clause applies to women; it applies to every person.

DECONCINI

First, let me just clarify this, Judge. You have stated that you now believe that the Fourteenth Amendment, the equal protection clause, applies to women. There is no question about that, is there, anymore?

BORK

None. It applies to everybody.

The equal protection clause applies to all racial discrimination, and I think about the only instance in which I have seen a court uphold a difference between races was when there was a race riot in a prison, and the warden separated the races, and somebody filed a lawsuit to challenge that. The court said that is reasonable. If there is a race riot, you can separate the races. That is the only instance I can recall. Otherwise, it is just about absolutely unconstitutional to make a racial distinction.

DECONCINI

I cannot understand then why the precise words used in the Fourteenth Amendment, which are "deny to any person within its jurisdiction the equal protection of the laws," creates the confusion that it does with you. It does not with me.

What words are not precise? If the plain language of the amendment requires States to equally protect all within its jurisdiction, why would there ever need to be any analysis of the legislative history or intent of the Congress when those words are as precise as this person can read them?

And I am not a student of the Constitution nor do I pretend to be a professional of constitutional law. The amendment does not say that the State cannot enact laws that discriminate. It says it must equally protect any person. Does this not mean that a State must enact laws to protect equally all persons? Is that not the rest of the amendment?

BORK

I think what it means is the State either by statute or by executive action, any way the State can act, may not deprive people of equal protection of the law. It does not mean that the State must go out affirmatively and legislate.

DECONCINI

But does it not mean it can go out affirmatively?

BORK

Sure. A State can affirmatively protect racial groups and other groups. There is no problem with that.

The historical meaning, the core idea, the trouble that caused the Fourteenth Amendment to be adopted was the fear of and the reality of racial discrimination against former slaves in this country, so that every time a court reasons about the Fourteenth Amendment it usually starts with the paradigm case of racial discrimination.

I objected to the Court using a method of saying this group, illegitimate children, aliens, is in; this group, somebody else, is out. That seemed to me to be a very funny way to proceed. We have no evidence that any of those groups were meant to be in or out. It is much better to proceed under the reasonableness test: everybody is covered, men, women, everybody.

And the question, when a statute makes a distinction, is whether the State has an adequate interest in it and the distinction is reasonable. Now in a racial case it will almost never be reasonable.

DECONCINI

Where do you find in this amendment that the reasonable standard is there, that it requires one standard here for racial and then another standard as you apply it other than racial?

BORK

The reasonable standard came in, I think, in the last century under the

Court, and I think that is a reasonable way to read this clause because it applies to all persons.

We know that it is irrational to make a distinction between persons on racial grounds, utterly irrational. We also know that for some purposes it is rational, reasonable to make a distinction between sexes.

DECONCINI

What troubles me is that you are saying that this reasonable test is something that the court has made up, that you are willing to use, and I do not see any distinction in that amendment. It seems to me far greater to say, "Yes, it applies to women, just as it applies to the races."

BORK

I said that, but it cannot apply just as it does to the races.

It is possible to say, for example, that there shall be no segregated toilet facilities anywhere as to race. I do not think anybody wants to say that as to gender. Differences have to be accommodated. That is why the difference.

DECONCINI

But is not that a bogus argument? We are not talking about unisex toilets here. We are talking about fundamental rights that women for too, too long have not been provided.

BORK

That is right.

DECONCINI

We are talking about your interpretation of whether or not on the Supreme Court you are going to look towards that equality for women, whether we have the Equal Rights Amendment or not. You have a reasonable standard that comes into play for women but you do not apply that reasonable standard to racial matters.

BORK

I do, Senator, I do. It is exactly the same standard.

DECONCINI

You do have the standard?

BORK

Yes, there is no reasonable basis to segregate the races by toilet facilities. There is a reasonable basis to segregate the genders by those facilities. When I said that you cannot treat gender exactly the same as you do race, all I meant was some distinctions are reasonable as to gender, such as the one we mentioned. The same would not be reasonable as to race.

The various things we would prohibit in the law as to race, not all of those would be prohibited as to gender. For example, you could not have a national law that said only blacks or only whites will go into combat. I do not want to arouse a philosophical argument here, but it certainly seems likely to me that you could have a national law — in fact, the Supreme Court has said as much — saying that only males will go into combat. There was a case about whether you could have an all-male draft, and the Court said you could.

That is an illustration that gender in some cases is treated differently from race.

SPECTER

Are you saying, then, that you will apply equal protection to women, just as the Court currently does?

BORK

Yes. I think a reasonable basis test gives you the same results as to gender that the Supreme Court has been reaching.

SPECTER

How about the strict scrutiny test, necessary to protect a compelling State interest?

BORK

That's what I was objecting to, Senator.

SPECTER

That's really the essence of equal protection, though, isn't it? If you use the reasonable basis test, a rational basis, pretty much everything is stricken. There is always something that can be conjured up as a rational basis?

BORK

No, no, Senator. They did that, and I objected to it in the Indiana article, because they begin to imagine rational bases.

I cited the cases critically in the Indiana article. They upheld the statute that said women couldn't be bartenders unless they were related to a male owner or proprietor of the bar. I thought that was a ridiculous distinction and I criticized it.

There are two methodologies. One is to say we will pick a group and say which level of scrutiny does it get. It is often said that race distinctions get strict scrutiny and require a compelling governmental interest.

Then there is intermediate scrutiny. Then there is rational basis, which is not what I'm talking about. Those are almost conclusions. You know if they get strict scrutiny, the statute is going to be struck down. You know if it gets rationality scrutiny, it's going to be upheld.

In the intermediate level of scrutiny, you don't know what they're going to do. There is no predictability to it.

I prefer to apply a reasonable basis test to all of those levels, and the result is that distinctions based on race almost never will be reasonable, except in the most urgent circumstances. Distinctions based upon gender will rarely be reasonable because, as we now view the place of women in society, only extreme cases based upon biological differences would probably be upheld. I mean, things like women in combat.

BIDEN

I can think of no test that would more violate the principle that you set out here than the reasonableness test, which is totally subjective. I think we both have to acknowledge that a judge — and I am not considering you conservative, liberal — can go anywhere he or she wants under that test. What is reasonable to me may be totally unreasonable to Senator Humphrey.

BORK

I can think of no test that is more subjective than the intermediate scrutiny test that the Court now uses. As a matter of fact, I was once arguing a case in the Supreme Court, and somebody said what about strict scrutiny. I said if you say strict scrutiny, the case is over. One of the other Justices said that is right, it is a conclusory term; we say strict scrutiny when we intend to strike it down.

In the past, they have said rationality when they intend to let it stand up. Intermediate scrutiny — nobody quite knows what that means. It goes all over the place, is highly subjective. I do not think the reasonable basis test is that subjective, but one could argue about which one is more subjective.

BIDEN

I believe the rational basis test is less subjective than the reasonableness test.

BORK

I do not like the multi-tier, group-by-group approach.

BIDEN

Well, I understand that. But doesn't it make sense in line with neutral principles and in keeping judges from wandering over the landscape to have the most objective test you can; and isn't the rational basis test more objective?

BORK

No. The rational basis test, if it is the lowest of the three tiers, is more objective only in the sense that it allows everything to be done. I mean, it just does not strike any laws down.

BIDEN

Isn't the embodiment of what you write that the Madisonian dilemma is resolved by saying that the only circumstances in which minorities have rights is when those rights are delegated to them by the majority. And the Constitution, really, is a gathering of the majority to enshrine in the Constitution what rights minorities will have; and that is why you have to look at the textual context of it, right?

BORK

That is right. The Constitution — the Bill of Rights, at least — was a great moment in which a super majority passed a self-denying law. That self-denying law has now been spread from the federal government to the State governments.

BIDEN

Let me stop you. There is the crux of your and my disagreement. I do not believe they were self-denying. That is why I think the Ninth Amendment meant something.

I think that the majority did not grant anything. What the majority did was acknowledge some of those rights that we automatically had that predated the Constitution, predated the Declaration of Independence, predated anything.

KENNEDY

It is clear from your public comments as recently as 3 months ago that you disapprove of the Supreme Court's recognition in the past 10 years that laws which discriminate on the basis of sex must be subject to heightened scrutiny under the Fourteenth Amendment, because under the rational basis test, the Supreme Court upholds a classification if it is rationally related to any government interest. That is a very lenient standard used by the courts in judging routine economic regulations that treat different persons and businesses differently.

In 1976 the Supreme Court rejected the rational basis test and applied a stricter standard for sex discrimination. Yet, in June of this year, you said that decision trivialized the Constitution. In this day and age men and women stand equal before the law. Women are first-class citizens, Mr. Bork, and your views would take us back to the days when women were second-class citizens and the Supreme Court winked at discrimination and denied equal rights for women.

BORK

In looking at the Fourteenth Amendment, race is the core of the amendment. That is what the post–Civil War amendments were basically aimed at. They wanted to help prevent discrimination against the newly freed slaves. Of course, race and ethnicity — that is the way the amendment was applied for a long time. It was applied to Chinese Americans in *Yick Wo v. Hopkins.*

At least for the last 90 years, roughly, the Court has also been doing two things. It has been using a reasonable basis test, but it has also engaged in the activity you described, by saying this group is in under the Fourteenth Amendment, that group is out.

Then they would develop multi-tier levels of scrutiny. That is, racial discrimination or distinction required strict scrutiny by the courts and a compelling governmental interest. Gender began to get intermediate scrutiny or something of that sort. I think that approach is highly artificial and not sufficient. I think you do not have to say this group is in, that group is out. You say that all persons are in, as the amendment does, and then you apply a reasonable basis test.

The reasonable basis test got a bad name because it simply is not applied with any degree of severity at all in economic cases, and maybe it should not be. Maybe those are interest group politics cases. But if you ask yourself whether a reasonable basis for distinction exists, the answer will be in a race case, almost never. In a gender case you will get something that resembles intermediate scrutiny, but you do not have to go through putting groups in and out and you do not have to have different tiers of scrutiny.

Women were not thought of as protected in particular when the Fourteenth Amendment was applied. There was a lot of what we now call discrimination against women which seemed to them a very natural way for civilization to be organized. But as the culture changes and as the position of women in society changes, those distinctions which seemed reasonable now seem outmoded stereotypes and they seem unreasonable and they get struck down.

That is the way a reasonable basis test should be applied.

KENNEDY

The point, Judge Bork, is that the rational basis test was the test the Supreme Court used for 100 years to deny equality for women. Some years ago the Court altered that to a rigorous standard for sex discrimination. As I understand the rational basis test, it is the same test which is used in terms of economic regulations and pollution ordinances. You have restated earlier in your response to Chairman Biden that this is still your test whereas the Court itself has moved to a much more rigorous standard to sex discrimination.

BORK

I do not think in the case of gender, Senator, that what you call my test, which is a test the Court has been applying in one way or another for 90 years, would come out that much different than an intermediate scrutiny standard.

KENNEDY

It was still the test that was used when women were discriminated against back in 1896. That was the basis and you get a very substantial body of legal opinion, plus the Justices, that believe that the test has been altered and changed to a rigorous standard test and that does provide a great deal more protection to women.

What I hear you saying is that the test that was used about 90 years ago and which was the basis for discrimination is the standard that you would use. You might be able to elaborate on it, but that is, at least, what I am hearing.

BORK

I do not know that it was the basis for discrimination against women. I think that society saw all kinds of legal distinctions between men and women as entirely reasonable and rational. This society no longer sees them that way, and that is fine.

DECONCINI

Now, I am trying to find out where you draw the line in your reasonable test, and I have not found that out, and if you could help me in a few words, it would be helpful.

BORK

Let me give you a couple of cases using what I consider the strict or the higher level of scrutiny which struck down the statutes in question. The dissent in these cases said the rational basis test should have been used and the statute should have been upheld. One is *Frontiero v. Richardson*, a 1973 case. Under the statute a serviceman could claim his wife as a dependent for the purpose of obtaining increased living allowance, medical and dental benefits without regard to whether she was, in fact, dependent upon him or any part of her support was dependent upon him. But a service woman may not claim a husband as a dependent for such purposes unless he could prove that half of his support was dependent on her. That case was decided 8 to 1 with Rehnquist writing the dissent.

Another case very near to that is *Kaban v. Muhammed*, 1979. Under that statute, a mother but not the father of an illegitimate child could block the adoption of a child by withholding the consent. That was a 4 to 5 decision with Justice Powell writing that.

DECONCINI

Comparing these two cases and comparing that rational test that was applied to both of these cases, I understand that the dissent used that rational, quote, "reasonable" test which you said is what you used. Is your view of the rational basis test different from the dissenters in these two cases or is that what it is, and if it is, I understand it. It doesn't throw you out of the Supreme Court as far as I'm concerned.

What I want to know is where you are.

BORK

No, you can use heightened scrutiny, intermediate scrutiny and lower scrutiny, or you can use the reasonable basis test.

DECONCINI

The reasonable basis test doesn't fall in any of these three in your judgement?

BORK

No. It is a different methodology.

DECONCINI

Okay.

BORK

And people who use heightened scrutiny on a particular case may come out different ways. People who use intermediate scrutiny may come out different ways. It is a matter of judgment.

Similarly, people who use the reasonable basis test may come out different ways. You know, it is like original intent. That doesn't give you a mechanical answer. What it does is get you into where you are starting from. That is all.

DECONCINI

So I did misunderstand you. I gathered that your reasonable standard on cases involving gender discrimination was similar to the rational basis. That is not the case?

BORK

No. No, it is not the lowest level of scrutiny.

DECONCINI

Okay. Now, is the reasonable standard test a fourth test?

BORK

It is an entirely different methodology.

DECONCINI

We are talking about heightened, intermediate, rational, and now reasonable?

BORK

No, it is an entirely different methodology. Instead of saying what degree of scrutiny is this group entitled to when a statute disadvantages them, it asks, is the differentiation, the disadvantage, made reasonable in light of a valid governmental purpose?

I would think as far as gender is concerned you could get, using a reasonable basis test, results at least as favorable to women as you would using intermediate scrutiny. I made a point in one of my decisions, the *Ollman* case, of saying that as society evolves constitutional doctrine will change, but it changes in certain ways.

The kinds of distinctions between men and women that are now allowable because reasonable are almost entirely based upon biological differences.

DECONCINI

Isn't that the same as rational?

BORK

You know, I don't know if it is the same as rational or not, but I am telling you the level at which I apply it. There are only a few things in life as to which a biological difference makes a difference.

DECONCINI

Otherwise, you would apply the intermediate or the strict interpretation, or test standard?

BORK

I was trying to get away from a methodology under which each group has its own level of scrutiny because I remember teaching this stuff in law school, and at one point we had two and a half levels or three and a half levels of scrutiny. It becomes highly artificial.

It is better to look at it and say this law makes a distinction, does it make any sense? There was a time in this country when the distinction made in *Frontiero*, that a woman is a dependent and a man is not, might have made some sense. That was a time when women were not in the marketplace so they would have to prove that they were in the marketplace.

That distinction now makes no sense because women are heavily into the marketplace, into careers. Hence, the result in *Frontiero* follows.

DECONCINI

But, in *Frontiero*, the facts are that Rehnquist used the rational basis test.

BORK

As I recall his testimony here before this committee, I think he is using the multi-tiers of analysis, strict scrutiny. He is using rational basis as the third and lowest level of scrutiny in these tiers. I am not even in that game.

DECONCINI

So you are not going to take to the Court, if you are confirmed, these three tiers?

BORK

No.

DECONCINI

You are going to take one tier? Both as to gender discrimination cases and race discrimination cases?

BORK

True.

DECONCINI

You won't apply the strict interpretation to the race discrimination test?

BORK

Well, in race—

DECONCINI

You are going to use reasonableness on everything is what you are saying

BORK

Yes. But in race, almost no distinction I can think of is reasonable.

This rationality test led them to say that women couldn't be licensed as bartenders unless they are related to a male proprietor. It just isn't much of a test. I think the Court got off on the wrong foot because they adopted the approach of what is known as Footnote 4 in the *Carolene Products* case, which says we must protect discrete and insular minorities, minorities who are small, don't have much contact or connection with the rest of the society, and aren't big enough to vote.

If you approach the equal protection clause in that way, women would not be covered, because women are not a discrete and insular minority.

BIDEN

Because they can vote.

BORK

This group-by-group approach, each group with a different standard, intermediate, etcetera, is really intellectually incoherent. The subjectivity of a reasonable-basis approach is no greater than much of constitutional law, and all the doctrine of neutral principles means is not that we have an automatic rule. It means that the judge should honestly say: "if I decide this case on these criteria, then I must decide any other case that has the same criteria the same way."

But this group-by-group approach, in which some groups get really no protection because they call it "rationality" and away we go, I think is wrong, because a lot of groups that are now covered in one way or another would never be covered if you went back to what they were aiming at.

BIDEN

They were aiming only at race, right?

BORK

Well, that was sure the core of it. If you are doing an original-understanding approach to the Constitution, the surest guide, the first thing you turn to, is the text, and the text of this thing says "nor shall any person be denied equal protection of the laws." That means that you don't say maybe they were thinking about blacks, former slaves, and so forth, but they stated a principle that's broader. I'm not so sure they were thinking about that. Maybe. I don't know. The language and the history suggest that this group-by-group approach is misguided.

Congressman Bingham, the drafter of the equal protection clause, when he was speaking to the Congress in support of it, said "Is it not essential to the unity of the government and the unity of the people that all persons, whether citizens or strangers within this land, shall have equal protection in every state?" And then there was Senator Howard, a member of the committee that drafted the Fourteenth Amendment, and its manager on the Senate floor, and he said "The equal protection clause abolishes all class legislation in the states and does away with the injustice of subjecting one caste of persons to a code not applicable to another."

I think it's more faithful to the language, and at least to what Senator Howard and Congressman Bingham said, to say this thing applies to all people, to any person; there is no reason to say this group gets this scrutiny, this group gets this scrutiny; it is much easier to say we are going to ask whether a distinction made between persons is a reasonable way to accomplish a valid legislative purpose. That means that the law is going to change over time. That is, understanding of reasonableness changes over time in the society.

BIDEN

Do you keep strict scrutiny in your test.

BORK

You get the same result as strict scrutiny, but you don't start with strict, intermediate, and —

BIDEN

So for you there is only one test, not strict, but just reasonable.

BORK

That is right. That is what Justice Stevens suggested with a great deal of merit.

CHAPTER SEVEN

BORK'S CLOSING
STATEMENT

Late in the afternoon of Saturday, September 21, the last question was asked, the Senators recapitulated their positions regarding the nomination, and Chairman Biden asked Bork if he wished to make a closing statement. At this point the outcome was still in doubt. The hearings would continue for the rest of the month, and the intensity of the campaign for and against the nominee would mount.

The votes of two key Senators remained undecided: Heflin, an Alabama Democrat and former chief justice of that state's supreme court, and Specter. While their two votes for Bork would leave the committee split 7–7, their support for confirmation would carry great weight in a final vote on the Senate floor.

Bork's closing statement reflects on the charge of a "confirmation conversion" and the view, as expressed by one Senator, that his vacillation left doubt as to where he now stood and where he would be on these issues if confirmed.

THE STATEMENT

Mr. Chairman, members of the committee, this has been a long, detailed, and often a profoundly interesting four and a half days of hearings. And I want to thank you personally Mr. Chairman for the courtesies you have personally extended to me and to my family during this week.

I also want to thank all the members of the committee for their patience, their attention, and their general good humor throughout these proceedings. For that I am most deeply grateful.

I have over the past four and a half days been asked a number of probing, highly complex and thoughtful questions covering a very broad range of subjects. I have answered those questions truthfully, openly and to the fullest extent possible without crossing the line that would place me in a position of speaking to specific matters that might come before either court.

If you have noted, there are views I have testified to here that reaffirm my acceptance of a body of jurisprudence as established and no longer judicially assailable, notwithstanding, that has developed in a manner different from a direction I had suggested some years ago. At the same time, there is much in my earlier writings — most particularly, my views on the proper role of judges and the need for faithful adherence to the text and the discernible intentions of the ratifiers of the Constitution and statutes — that I subscribe to just as fully today as I did before.

As a consequence, I have received criticism in some quarters for being too rigid and criticism in other quarters for being inconsistent or self-contradictory. Neither charge is, in my opinion, an accurate one. As I said to you in my opening statement, I am a jurist who believes his role is to interpret the law and not to make it.

If the members of the committee are looking, as you have said you are, for predictability, it is certainly predictable that I will adhere to my judicial philosophy as I have described it in these hearings and elsewhere. That may lead on occasion to results that conservatives applaud and on other occasions to results that liberals applaud, but in either event it will not be because of some personal political agenda of my own. It will not be a desire to set a social agenda for the nation. It will be because the result, in my considered judgment, is required by the law.

On that point, let me simply add, as I also did in my opening statement, that when I say "the law," I regard precedent as an important component of the law. As I have described many times here, there are a number of important precedents that are today so woven into the fabric of our system that to change or alter them would be, in my view, unthinkable.

Mr. Chairman and members of the committee, you have my record before you. It shows not only a full sensitivity toward minorities and women, but a consistent record favoring the interests of minorities and women. I have given you my full view of the equal protection clause. It means what the words say: all persons are protected against unreasonable legislative classifications.

You have heard me testify under oath, and I take an oath as a very serious and affirmative thing. I have affirmed my full acceptance of the Supreme Court's First Amendment jurisprudence, including the *Brandenburg* decision, and I have affirmed my full acceptance of the incorporation doctrine, and there are many other areas in which that is true.

I have tried to be responsive to your questions. I hope I have succeeded. But to the extent any members have further questions, I will be glad to answer them at a later time.

Again, Mr. Chairman, I want to thank you and the members of this committee.

EPILOGUE

On October 6, by a vote of 9 (Biden, Byrd, DeConcini, Heflin, Kennedy, Leahy, Metzenbaum, Simon, and Specter) to 5 (Grassley, Hatch, Humphrey, Simpson, and Thurmond) the committee voted to recommend to the Senate that the nomination be rejected. Over the next few days pressure mounted for Bork to withdraw his name to avoid a losing fight on the Senate floor. He refused. On October 23, 58 senators voted against confirmation. The Bork nomination was dead, but those truly interested had experienced a once-in-a-lifetime event, a full-scale, weeklong examination of the U.S. Constitution by some of the most prominent names in American politics.

The confirmation hearings in early 1988 for Anthony Kennedy, Powell's ultimate replacement, partially confirmed Senator Simpson's prediction that such a probing, exhaustive interrogation of a Supreme Court nominee would not be repeated. Kennedy was on the witness stand briefly. His entire hearing took two and a half days, with little opposition. For whatever reason, no one desired to sit through the legal seminar again.

SUGGESTIONS FOR
FURTHER READING

For additional reading on the Bork nomination, see Ethan Bronner, *Battle for Justice: How the Bork Nomination Shook America* (New York: W.W. Norton Co., 1989); Robert H. Bork, *The Tempting of America: The Political Seduction of the Law* (New York: The Free Press, 1989); and *Nomination of Robert H. Bork to be Associate Justice of the Supreme Court of the United States: Hearings Before the Senate Committee on the Judiciary*, 100th Cong., 1st Sess. (Washington, D.C.: G.P.O., 1989). Also important on the Bork nomination are works by Senator Paul Simon, a member of the Judiciary Committee, *Advice and Consent: Clarence Thomas, Robert Bork, and the Intriguing History of the Supreme Court's Nomination Battles* (Washington, D.C.: National Press Books, 1992), and Norman Vieira and Leonard Gross, *Supreme Court Appointments: Judge Bork and the Politicization of Senate Confirmations* (Carbondale: Southern Illinois University Press, 1998).

Two brilliant constitutional scholars deeply influenced Bork: Alexander M. Bickel, *The Supreme Court and the Idea of Progress* (New York: Harper and Row, 1970), and Raoul Berger, *Government by Judiciary: The Transformation of the Fourteenth Amendment*, 2nd ed. (Indianapolis: Liberty Fund, 1997).

One of the most important volumes on original intent is Leonard Levy's *Original Intent and the Framers' Constitution* (New York: Macmillan, 1988), which also discusses judicial review, precedent, the Ninth Amendment, and the Bill of Rights. See also Joseph M. Lynch, *Negotiating the Constitution: The Earliest Debates over Original Intent* (Ithaca, N.Y.: Cornell University Press, 1997), covering the period from the Constitutional Convention through the Virginia and Kentucky Resolutions, and Keith E. Whittington, *Constitutional Interpretation: Textual Meaning, Original Intent, and Judicial Review* (Lawrence: University Press of Kansas, 1999).

Harold J. Spaeth and Jeffrey A. Segal, *Majority Rule or Minority Will: Adherence to Precedent on the U.S. Supreme Court* (Cambridge: Cambridge University Press, 1999), traces changing positions on precedent from John Marshall to the Rehnquist Court. John Agresto, *The Supreme Court and Constitutional Democracy* (Ithaca, N.Y.: Cornell University Press, 1984), concentrates on judicial review. Separation of powers is the subject of Kermit Hall's *The Least Dangerous Branch: Separation of Powers and Court-packing* (New York: Garland Publ., 2000).

Incorporation theory—extending the protection guaranteed by the Bill of Rights to actions by states as well as by the national government—is a subject of Charles Fairman and Stanley Morrison, *The Fourteenth Amendment and the Bill of Rights: The Incorporation Theory* (New York: Da Capo Press, 1970). Randy E. Barnett, *The Rights Retained by the People: The History and Meaning of the Ninth Amendment* (Fairfax, Va.: George Mason University Press, 1989), and Marshall L. DeRosa, *The Ninth Amendment and the Politics of Creative Jurisprudence: Disparaging the Fundamental Right of Popular Control* (New Brunswick, N.J.: Transaction Publishers, 1996), offer insight into the role of unspecified rights.

Privacy and abortion are the subject of David J. Garrow, *Liberty and Sexuality: The Right to Privacy and the Making of Roe v. Wade* (New York: Macmillan, 1994).

For a general history of the United States Supreme Court, see the official volume published in association with the Supreme Court Historical Society: Robert Shnayerson, *The Illustrated History of the Supreme Court of the United States* (New York: Harry N. Abrams, Inc., 1986).

About the Editor

Ralph E. Shaffer is professor of history, emeritus, at California State Polytechnic University, Pomona, where he taught from 1963 to 1993 and served as department chairman from 1975 to 1979. He is the editor of *Which Path to Freedom? The Black Anti-Slavery Debate, 1815–1860* and *Toward Pearl Harbor: The Diplomatic Exchange between Japan and the United States, 1899–1941.* His online books, found at http://www.csupomona.edu/~reshaffer/, are *Letters from the People: The Los Angeles Times Letters Column, 1881–1889* (1999–2000) and *California and the Coming of the Fifteenth Amendment,* vol. 2, *Implementing the Fifteenth Amendment in California: 1870* (2005). He is a frequent contributor to the op-ed pages of various California newspapers, including the *Los Angeles Daily News* and the *Los Angeles Times.*

www.ingramcontent.com/pod-product-compliance
Lightning Source LLC
Chambersburg PA
CBHW020612270326
41927CB00005B/301